Pumpkin Farm tray - 16 in
Ash base inlaid with poplar, blackberry, pernambuco, mahogany, apple, purple sandcherry, pear, moradillo

Floral Fruit tray - 16 in
American cherry base inlaid with purpleheart, amarillo, caragana, tulip poplar, greenheart, moradillo, pernambuco, satinwood, osage orange, Brazilian rosewood, padauk, Honduran mahogany, black walnut, birch, Ceylon ebony, hackberry, tulipwood

Cottage Garden tray - 20 in
Birch base inlaid with poplar, mahogany, apple, locust, Brazilian rosewood, black walnut, pernambuco, purpleheart, greenheart, gumwood, Russian olive, maple, moradillo, caragana, tulipwood, osage orange, amarillo, padauk, Ceylon ebony, hackberry

A calendar with a scene I admire, a greeting card, the design in a rug, or a still-life arrangement all feed my imagination and form the basis of my patterns, which can be varied according to the wood available and the project undertaken.

To make the projects in this book I suggest beginning with the napkin holder or vegetable wall plaque then the bulrush plaque, which introduce the basic techniques, and then proceed to the more advanced round box with acorns and the double inlay technique of the holly leaves. As you progress you will find pattern sources everywhere to use for your own inlay ideas. Pages 1-5 show the variety of designs that can be created and you can copy these or make up your own. The theme of this book is not only of patterns and projects but of concepts and ideas that can be developed through the techniques outlined in this book.

🌿 Getting Started 🌿

Work Space

You will need a special place to do your inlay work. A workbench that suits your height is ideal (mine is 36 in high). On this I have a work platform 16 in x 7 in x 4 in high, which is weighted on the underside with a plate of steel 1 in x 6 in x 16 in which acts as an anvil block. This keeps the platform in place and allows the chisel to make cuts easily and cleanly. This platform is easily moved on the workbench to any position. Cover the platform with a soft durable material — cardboard works well. This absorbs the wood chips that get under the project and prevents the project wood from being scratched or chipped. Good lighting is essential over the working area. A magnifying lamp is useful as well.

Workshop shows bench area and work platform with overhead magnifying light

❧ Being Careful ❧

Safety is an important aspect of woodworking and the work area should be set up with this in mind. All power tools should be operated according to the manufacturer's instructions and kept away from children. Never use any electrical tool or machine whose plug has been damaged. Make sure all tools are electrically grounded where required. Routers are powerful cutting machines and must be handled carefully. I use power tools mainly for making the base pieces. They are convenient but not essential. Cutting tools such as chisels must be kept sharp. Dull tools cause accidents.

It's a good idea to wear a covering apron to protect clothing and prevent loose garments from being caught in machinery. Sleeves can be rolled up when using power tools. Safety shoes and glasses and a dust mask are also a good idea.

Keeping the work area clean prevents damage to the project

Be sure to keep the work area clean so that wood chips do not damage the project. Remove large wood chips with a shop vacuum and have vacuum outlet ports attached to power sanding and power sawing equipment to draw up minute sawdust particles. Sawdust sticks to hands and clothing so remove apron and work clothes before entering other parts of the house. Be knowledgeable about the wood you use. Some woods are toxic and can cause serious health problems when the sawdust is breathed in. I found that I am allergic to sumac. Be cautious when you are working with new woods. Try one at a time to determine your reaction.

❧ Woods to Consider ❧

Only small amounts of wood are needed for inlay material. Some can be purchased at lumber yards and from fine wood suppliers. You can also collect your own supply of special wood from branches and roots of fallen trees that can be interesting for inlay work. I keep a variety of wood pieces in buckets to have on hand when I need them. They are dry and ready for use. These are my "paints" to create my inlay pictures.

American crab apple This wood is generally available and very decorative but dulls tools and is difficult to work with. It yields nearly white sapwood and almost walnut-brown heartwood.

Apple Fruit bearing trees are generally available and yield very light sapwood and light brown heartwood.

Ash White or American ash is most common and is easily worked. It has a yellowish-white color.

Aspen This wood works well and has a whitish-yellow color.

Birch This wood has wavy grain patterns, spalts beautifully, and often grows spectacular burls. It can be almost iridescent when polished. Color varies from light yellow-brown to deep reddish-brown.

Black bean This imported wood is olive green with dark stripes.

Black locust A yellowish-brown wood which is very hard. Honey locust is creamier in color.

Bloodwood First choice for a deep, dark red color. Available at specialty stores. Also called cardinal wood.

Box elder This member of the soft maple family is prized by woodworkers because of the fungus-caused pink coloring, and often has a red-and-tan marble wood pattern.

Caragana This Siberian pea tree shrub produces branches that can be utilized for their yellow color.

Northern white cedar This wood is commonly available, grows burls, and has elegant grain patterns.

Western red cedar This straight-grained wood is commonly available, grows elegant burls, and is aromatic; however it is highly toxic and can cause serious health problems to woodworkers if dust is breathed in.

The
Art *of*
Wood Inlay
Projects & Patterns

George Stevens

Sterling Publishing Co., Inc. New York
A Sterling/Tamos Book

A Sterling/Tamos Book
© 2005 George Stevens

Sterling Publishing Co., Inc.
387 Park Avenue South
New York, NY 10016-8810

Tamos Books Inc.
300 Wales Avenue
Winnipeg, MB Canada R2M 2S9

10 9 8 7 6 5 4 3 2 1

Distributed in Canada by Sterling Publishing
c/o Canadian Manda Group, 165 Dufferin Street
Toronto, Ontario, Canada M6K 3H6
Distributed in Great Britain by Chrysalis Books Group PLC
The Chrysalis Building, Bramley Road, London W10 6SP, England
Distributed in Australia by Capricorn Link (Australia) Pty. Ltd.
P.O. Box 704, Windsor, NSW 2756, Australia

Design S. Fraser & A. Crawford
Photography Jerry Grajewski, Grajewski Fotograph Inc.,

Library and Archives Canada Cataloging in Publication
Stevens, George, 1944-
        The art of wood inlay : projects and patterns / George Stevens.
Includes index.
ISBN 1-895569-82-6
                1. Marquetry--Technique. I.Title.
TT192.S75 2004   745.51'2   C2004-907200-5

Library of Congress Cataloging-in-Publication Data
Stevens, George.
  The art of wood inlay / George Stevens.
    p. cm.
  "A Sterling/Tamos Book."
  Includes index.
  ISBN 1-895569-82-6
  1. Marquetry. I. Title.

TT192.S74 2005
745.51'2--dc22

                                        2005001057

Tamos Books Inc. acknowledges the financial support of the Government of
Canada through the Book Publishing Development Program (BPIDP) for our
publishing activities.

The advice and directions given in this book have been carefully checked, prior
to printing, by the Author as well as the Publisher. Nevertheless, no guarantee
can be given as to the project outcome due to the possible differences in
materials. Author and Publisher will not be responsible for the results.

ISBN 1-895569-82-6

For information about custom editions, special sales, premium and
corporate purchases, please contact Sterling Special Sales
Department at 800-805-5489 or specialsales@sterlingpub.com.

Author
John George Allan Stevens was born in Winnipeg, Canada in
1944. He worked throughout Northern Manitoba and across
the Canadian Arctic for many years before returning to
Winnipeg where he now resides. His life-long passion for wood
led him to hobby woodworking which evolved into the special
craft of inlay where he is able to showcase wood in its natural
splendor. The extent of wood's possibilities for inlay art was
enhanced when he had the opportunity to purchase two truck
loads of wood cut-offs and shorts from a local lumber yard. The
great variety of colors and textures was all the inspiration he
needed to create a wide range of inlay pictures. How to use
wood to its best advantage to show off nature's bounty remains
his special interest.

Acknowledgements
Many people assisted me in putting this book together and I
would like to thank my wife Marvee for her love and support,
also my daughter Kimberly Almond and her husband Mike
Muehe, my son Chad Stevens, my niece Paula Ehn, Joanne
Deslauriers, my friend Ron Beek, and my son Jamie Almond
who enjoys working with wood and does all the finishing on all
my pieces. Thanks are also extended to all my family and
friends who encouraged me and assisted in many ways. Without
their support this book would not have been possible. I am
grateful to Jamie Almond (p5), Fred and Roxanne Schlorff (p5),
Glen and Colleen Macintyre (p1), and Alannah Almond-Muehe
(p4) for allowing me to photograph inlay pieces that I made
and gave to them.

My special thanks to my sister and brother-in-law,
Margaret and Eric Ehn.

❧ Table of Contents ❧

Preparatory

Introduction	4
Getting Started	5
Being Careful	6
Woods to Consider	6
Wood Grain	8
Tools	9
Tool Sharpening	11
Transferring Patterns	12
Inlay Press	13
Basic Inlay Steps	14
Making a Tight inlay	15
Drawing Leaves	15
Making Leaf Constructs	16
Preparing Inlay Pieces	17
Inlay Techniques	18
Picture Frame	18
Repairing Inlay	19
Finishing	20

Inlay Projects

Picture Frame	13
Napkin Holder	23
Vegetable Wall Plaque	26
Hanger Detail	27
Mushroom Paddle Trivet	29
Bulrush Plaques	32
Decorative Tiles	39
Candy Dish	43
Poinsettia Plaque	46
Lazy Susan	51
Trinket Boxes	55
Recipe Box	59
Recipe Book Stand	63
Watering Can Tray	67
Fruit Tray	71
Card Box	75
Teddy Bear Step Stool	78
Round Acorn Box	84
Earrings, Brooch, Bracelet	90
Walnut Tulip Plaque	93
Yellow Rose Plaque	97
Pin Tray	103
Christmas Ornaments	107
Lily Bed Tray	114
Nested Bowls	122
Finishing Charts	126
Metric Conversion	128
Index	128

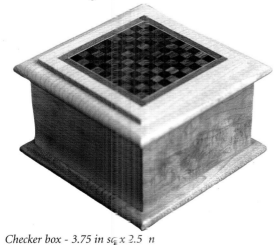

Checker box - 3.75 in sq x 2.5 in
Maple base inlaid with
mahogany and maple

Grain and floral tray on title page - 16 in
Elm base inlaid with caragana, plum root,
hackberry, purpleheart, pernambuco, mahogany,
amarillo, tulip poplar

🍂 Introduction 🍂

In the visual arts, inlay offers its creator the opportunity to make beautiful pictures — flowers, scenes, figures — without the medium of paint. The creator makes the design from cut out pieces of variously colored, or elaborately grained, or specialty wood or materials such as precious metals, leather, or mother-of-pearl, and sets them into the main structure that is hollowed out to receive them. The resulting inlay work is not only decorative but can achieve depth, perspective, and texture as well by the choice and placement of the various inlaid materials.

Inlay techniques have been practiced for a long time. Beautiful red lacquered boxes inlaid with carved mother-of-pearl designs were important pieces in the Ming dynasty in China and later in the Ch'ing dynasty where the inlay workmanship achieves exquisite artistry. Japan, too, favored this art and its black lacquered boxes set with mother-of-pearl designs dating from the 8th Century are exceptional. Some inlay was done on lacquered tables and cabinets as well and these household items greatly influenced European furniture-making. Inlay techniques were widely used by European craftsmen and are still practiced today by some artisans, although furniture-making has gradually adopted marquetry and veneering to do the decorative designs. These skills are sometimes compared to inlay but the process is completely different. In marquetry the decorative patterns that are created from other materials are applied to the surface of the base piece, forming an additional layer of material that incorporates the design.

Inlay today seems to be a forgotten art. Fewer and fewer examples of this remarkable craft are available and not much information about the techniques exists. My interest grew from my love of wood and my skills have developed over a lifetime of making patterns and fitting together beautiful pieces of wood to create my designs. Different kinds of wood offer so much variety of color and richness of texture for my art that this medium is more than adequate for me to "paint" my pictures.

Over the years I have become a collector of wood and I attend every tree trimming and tree excavating that I know about in my neighborhood. When I see an interesting piece I immediately plan how I could use it in my inlay designs. For me, an old root or a caragana branch from my neighbor's hedge are the source of infinite joy. I search out discarded branches from Russian olive trees, old cedar shingles, and many other woods not harvested for commercial use. The beauty of such pieces is often a surprise and proves more interesting than wood found in lumber yards, although I raid these places too. Choosing wood and working with it give me great pleasure and I use my inlay creations as a showcase for nature's bounty of beautiful wood. Inlay design can accent any woodworking project and it is an easy and inexpensive way to make plain pieces special.

The craft of wood inlay is not difficult to learn and can be accomplished with a minimum of tools that are likely already in your workshop. A sharp knife and an assortment of chisels are the main items. The objective is to hollow out a cavity in a particular piece of wood the exact size required to accept the inlay. In this book I present 24 projects that range from simple to more elaborate and include step-by-step instructions of the various techniques needed to make these pieces. I've also included patterns that can be copied for the designs plus a listing of woods that I used for the construction. As you work with different woods you may choose some that are more available to you or that offer the colors you need for your creation. The patterns I chose came from many different sources.

Cradle - Maple and American cherry base inlaid with tulip poplar, moradillo, purpleheart, caragana, amarillo, osage orange, pernambuco, Philippine mahogany, plum root, Ceylon ebony, cherry, birch

Ceylon ebony This imported wood is black interspersed with shades of brown, purple, and gray.

Chakte kok This wood is reddish with black streaks. The end grain has a swirl pattern.

Cherry This fine-textured wood has reddish-brown heartwood with brown flecks and lighter sapwood. American cherry is lighter than European cherry.

Cocobolo This member of the rosewood family buffs to a shiny finish, is durable, and maintains reddish color. The wood is safe but the sawdust if breathed in can cause a toxic shock reaction.

Crystobal Wood has reddish-brown to violet heartwood, creamy sapwood. Also called granadillo.

Greenheart This imported wood is brown with an occasional green shade.

Gumwood This wood is often called satin walnut. It is milk brown, can be nicely marked.

Hackberry This wood of the elm family has yellow to grayish sapwood and yellowish gray-brown heartwood.

Holly Commonly available holly is the whitest known wood. Has a fine grain. Heartwood is cream-white, often with a greenish-gray cast, the sapwood is white or light tan. Black-dyed holly is sometimes sold as ebony.

Laburnum This imported wood has a strong grain and rich olive green color.

Laurel This imported wood is handsomely figured and is colored warm yellow to brown.

Magnolia Limited amount of wood harvested varies from green to reddish-brown.

Mahogany Commonly available, this wood is soft and works easily. It has deep brown to reddish color.

Maple There are many maples. Bird's Eye maple has bird's eye figuring and off-white color. Red maple has swirled grain patterns. Silver maple can be spalted, is off-white, and hard to finish. Sugar maple has elegant grain figures and is off-white, often with dark brown heart.

Moradillo This wood is reddish-orange with darker red to brown streaks.

Mulberry black and red Commonly available, has a rich yellow color that darkens over time to golden brown.

Red oak This coarse-textured wood varies from light cream, pinkish-red to dark tan or brown.

Oak Many different varieties are available. The wood is many shades of brown with a distinctive grain.

Russian olive This wood is brown and used for small woodwork projects.

Osage orange This yellow wood turns orangy-brown when exposed to light.

Padauk This wood is reddish-purple, darkens to a deep reddish-purple or grayish-black on exposure.

Pau amarillo First choice wood for a bright canary yellow color. Available through specialty stores.

Pao rosa Wavy grain has pink, yellow, or dark brown heartwood often striped with red-brown bands.

Pear This pale reddish-yellow wood has a short close grain and is a favorite for carvers.

Pernambuco This imported quality hardwood is used in furniture making. It has a red color.

Yellow pine Commonly available (also called white pine), the wood is soft but has interesting burls, crotches, and knots.

Jack pine This wood is gray with interesting knots.

Plum This nicely streaked wood is found in brownish or red.

Poplar This soft, fine-textured whitish wood turns green or gray when exposed to light. Also called tulip tree.

Purpleheart This wood is light brown when cut but turns purple on exposure. Also called amarant.

Redwood This wood comes from farmed source and has a reddish color.

Rhododendron Shrubs often develop wood burls which make them interesting for woodworking.

Rosewood This beautiful imported wood is dark purple-brown banded with striped markings.

Sandpaper wood This attractive wood is light brown and ideal to make mushrooms for inlay.

Satinwood One of the most beautiful woods known, is brown with an overcast of salmon, green, gray, and sometimes black bindings. Imported

Siberian elm This fairly brittle wood is a perfect light brown color to make mushrooms for inlay.

Staghorn sumac This "junk" plant has iridescent yellow-green wood that darkens slightly over time.

Sweet gum The sapwood is cream colored and the heartwood (commercially sold as American red green) varies from a satiny pinkish-brown to a deep red-brown.

Sycamore This imported wood is nearly milk-white and often richly mottled.

Tulipwood Hard dense wood has pinkish to yellowish heartwood with violet, salmon, and rose stripes.
Tupelo This wood has interlocked grain with gray-brown sapwood and darker heartwood.
Walnut This wood varies from tan to purple-brown/black (coarse texture but sands to a smooth satin finish).
Wenge The heartwood is dark brown with fine black veins and white lines. It has a straight grain.
Yellow willow This soft wood is a pale yellowish-gray color.
Yew Heartwood is orange-brown to golden-orange, streaked with purple and brown. Irregular grain pattern.
Zebra wood Heartwood has brown stripes running through creamy-yellowish background. Wood is stinky so wear a mask when working the wood. Imported from Africa

---

Burl is a wart-like growth on the side of a tree. It has a whorled grain.

Swirling occurs around knots and burls and provides an interesting grain pattern.

Spalting is a fungus that turns black or dark brown when it dries causing irregular lines in the wood.

Heartwood is the mature wood at the center of a tree that has stopped growing. It is a darker color than sapwood which is the outer portion of a tree next to the bark.

All these wood patterns can be used in interesting ways in woodworking projects.

🌿 Wood Grain 🌿

Finding a flat grain or edge grain cut of wood is not always on the edge or flat side of a piece of dressed lumber. Read the end grain of the piece of wood to find where the tree rings bisect the wood. Using the same cut of wood for like or similar inlay pieces is important since each cut of wood accepts a finish differently, so pieces that do not match may not look well in the design.

Collection of various wood pieces used for inlay

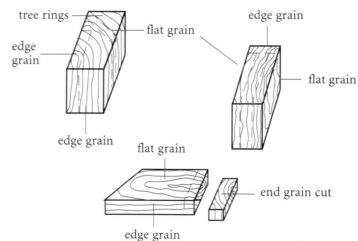

Wood Combinations   Color of wood and the grain make the piece interesting. Using all flat-grained cuts may make the picture busy because of the decorative grain pattern or the picture may look boring or flat if you use only edge-cut pieces. Mixing grain cuts adds as much interest as mixing wood colors. Although the pieces are very small, cutting them at random and inlaying them can result in unexpected effects. However, when you need to use a number of pieces that are equal in appearance, grain matters. When cutting and using small pieces of wood it is sometimes difficult to know what cut it is. If you cannot cut enough matching pieces from a single piece of wood whose grain cannot be defined, it would be wise to choose another piece. Although the edge grain or flat grain of a small piece of wood may look the same, each may take a finish differently. The results could make a difference in the appearance of the work.

The Art of Wood Inlay

🌿 Tools 🌿

I use a few power tools mostly to make the base objects into which I do my inlay work; however, hand tools work as well depending on what you have in your workshop.

Power Tools

These are some power tools that I find useful.

1. **Scroll saw** These saws come in a wide range of sizes, shapes, and qualities. Choose a size that you can operate comfortably.
2. **Table saw** A small 8 in bench-top model is adequate for this work.
3. **Jigsaw** Used to cut boards to a size easily managed in the scroll saw.
4. **Disk sander** Use this tool to shape and thickness small inlay pieces.
5. **Drill press, crow's foot and vise** A variety of sanding drums chucked into a drill press are used to shape the cutout pieces for the inlay.
6. **Router and router table** A ¼ in router with bits is sufficient for wood inlay.
7. **Thickness plane** Wood can be cut accurately and quickly to the correct thickness.

Electric Motors

Where there is an option, open winding electric motors should never be used for woodworking machines. If you are planning to purchase a motor for any of your woodworking machines a totally enclosed unit should always be your first choice. However, open winding, fractional horsepower motors are often salvaged in good condition from discarded appliances and you can utilize these motors in your workshop. These suggestions will help.

1. Always operate the motor in plain view, and do not place a cover over it so that you forget about it when you clean the shop.
2. Be sure to have a good dust collection system in place to prevent the accumulation of wood dust.
3. Do not mount it where it can accumulate wood dust from any other woodworking tool.
4. Never leave it running unattended.
5. Always clean and vacuum the inside of the motor daily. If you operate the motor with a switch make sure it is placed in a dust tight electrical box and fitted with a dust tight switch plate. I use an open winding motor for my disk sander and it is operated by plugging it into a wall outlet beside the unit, eliminating the need for a switch.

Scroll saw & table saw in work area *Jigsaw*

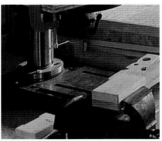

Sanding disk *Crow's foot & vise (drill press not visible)*

¼ in router *Thickness plane cuts thickness accurately*

Note Single phase fractional horsepower motors rely on an internal centrifugal switch to disengage the starting winding after the motor has reached its operating speed. The accumulation of wood dust will interfere with the operation of this switch and cause the motor to overheat within seconds posing a real fire hazard. The centrifugal switch is also a source of electrical arcing even under normal operation. If you suspect that any wood dust has accumulated over time within the motor it should be disassembled and thoroughly cleaned.

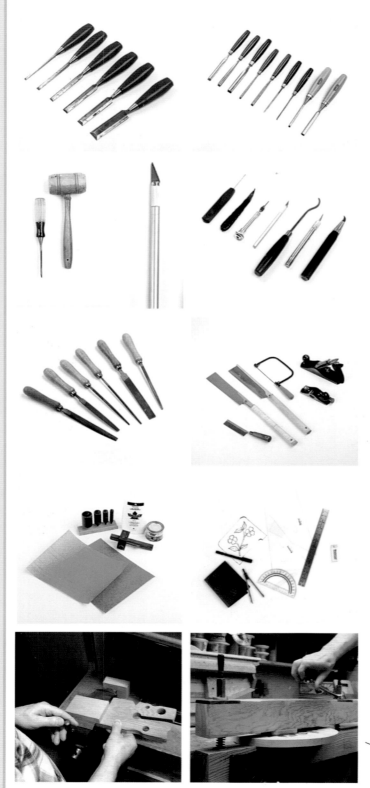

Inlay Tools

These are the tools I find indispensable for inlay work. Read from top, left to right.

1 **Flat chisels** A standard set of chisels from ⅛ in to 1 in wide is used to cut lines into the inlay cavity and remove wood.

2 **Curved chisels** Use curved chisels to carve round corners and remove wood from curved lines.

3 **Mallet and chisel** The wooden mallet and ⅛ in flat chisel are used for 90 percent of the vertical edges of inlay work.

4 **X-acto knife** The X-acto knife with #2 blade is my main cutting tool. I use it to scribe around the inlay pieces to make an accurate line to begin the inlay.

5 **Knives and scraping tools** I use a variety of knives and straight and curved scrapers to remove wood and smooth surfaces.

6 **Wood files** Use an assortment of small wood files to establish primary and secondary bevels on each inlay piece. Done with the help of a crow's foot.

7 **Small hand tools** A variety of fine-toothed saws, a smooth and block plane shown here help to cut inlays to size and planing thickness required.

8 **Miscellaneous supplies** You will need sandpaper in various grits, glue and wood filler, a marking gauge, and drum sanders.

9 **Drafting tools** You will need various drafting tools to transfer the patterns accurately to the inlay base and for the inlay pieces.

10 **Crow's foot** This bench tool is secured by clamp or #2 Record workman's bench vise model V175. It offers table support for small pieces of wood. Bench vise is standard shop tool.

11 **Inlay press & press block** Make your own press block in various sizes to suit projects. Place on top of inlay wood base before using inlay press.

12 **Bench hook** Use this to hold small wood pieces while working.

bench hook

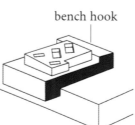

Note   Router bits used for projects in this book are carbide or carbide tipped. A finely sharpened carbide will cut easier for much longer than any high speed steel option. You will see the difference in the quality of the work.

🌿 Tool Sharpening 🌿

The sharper the tools the easier and safer it is to complete wood inlay work. For hobbyist woodworkers, however, it is often difficult to maintain a keen edge on knives and chisels. They never seem to be sharp enough. I find I can do quite well with just two basic bench stones, a diamond stone and a Japanese water stone. It also helps to keep a select group of chisels and knives for inlay work only. This makes them easy to maintain with a minimal amount of time involved in keeping them sharp. Most chisels when purchased are ground to a 25° angle which I find adequate. The paring chisel has a blade ground to an angle as low as 17°. The thinner edge of this chisel allows you to cut a clean vertical side to the inlay cavity, but this edge is more difficult to maintain and requires frequent sharpening.

Using the diamond stone to keep chisels sharp

Basic Maintenance

To maintain the blade angle, I use a medium 1200 grit diamond stone. An adjustable honing guide designed to hold straight-edged chisels at the correct angle while sharpening is also useful. Curved chisels must be sharpened freehand and it takes some practice to gain proficiency in freehand honing. Begin with a circular motion and then a few straight strokes. After the basic bevel has been established, the back of the blade should be rubbed flat on the stone to remove any wire edge that may have resulted from honing the bevel. The primary bevel can then be established. Use the diamond stone to make the primary bevel which should be $\frac{1}{16}$ in to $\frac{1}{8}$ in wide, ground onto the leading edge of the chisel at an angle of one or two degrees less than the established angle.

A 4000-grit waterstone will hone this bevel to a very keen edge. Remove any burrs by lapping the back of the chisel placed flat on the stone. This edge is not keen enough for wood carving but is quite adequate for inlay work. Do not allow the primary bevel to become too wide because it will take longer to achieve a keen edge. If it does become too wide re-establish the basic bevel on the diamond stone and start a new primary bevel. The use of small shaped slipstones is needed to assist in honing curved gouge chisels.

Diamond sharpening stones can be used without any lubricant, but a little water helps to keep them keen. Because they cut aggressively, wipe them clean frequently to remove abraded metal. Reapply a little water and continue. Avoid sharpening tools that are covered in oil or resin. This will clog the stone. To clean the stone use a fine wire brush. The keenness of any edge will always depend upon the size of grit in the stone or the abrasive powder used to hone the final edge of the tool.

To scribe inlay shapes and cut shoulders I use a #2 blade made by X-acto tools. The stainless steel version is very strong and sharp. However, after inlaying just one or two pieces of wood the tip of this blade (about $\frac{1}{32}$ in) will break off. This loss does not detract from the blade's usefulness. In fact, all the inlay projects for this book were completed with just two blades, usually minus tips. These blades are not expensive and are easily replaced. Sharpening this knife blade is not a real issue, but the sharpened edge is not as good as when it was new.

> **Grinding** To sharpen knives or chisels it is not necessary to grind the edge unless it is nicked or significantly dulled in some way. If grinding is necessary do not overheat the edge because this will cause the steel to lose its temper and the tool will not sustain a sharp edge. A 1/4 horsepower (1,725 rpm) double spindle grinder will give good results. Using an aluminum oxide wheel on the grinder will help to keep the edge cool. Frequently dipping the blade in a water bath is also a good strategy.

🍂 Transferring Pattern 🍂

The patterns in this book can be photocopied to size on thin cardboard or clear acetate and cut out to use as a template for making the inlay pieces from selected woods (see Method 1). To make inlay pattern on base piece see Method 2.

Method 1 Inlay Pieces

Read photos from top, left to right.

1 Plane inlay piece to desired thickness.
2 Photocopy pattern to size required. Shows wood selected for particular inlay piece paying attention to grain pattern and color.
3 Lay carbon paper on wood inlay piece and place inlay piece pattern on top.
4 Trace around pattern of inlay piece with pencil.
5 Pattern of inlay piece transferred to wood ready to cut out.
6 Cut out inlay piece along traced line.
7 Piece is now ready to inlay.

Alternative Method for Inlay Pieces

1 Plane inlay piece to desired thickness.
2 From a drafting supply store purchase a clear acetate.
3 Place the acetate over the required drawing that has been photocopied to size and trace the pattern with a fine tipped pen. Mark the grain direction and wood choice on the pattern piece. Use as a template to make inlay piece OR place carbon paper over chosen inlay wood, cover with desired pattern, and trace inlay pattern piece onto inlay wood.

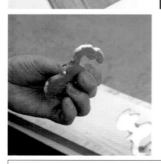
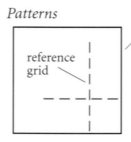
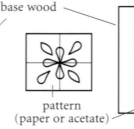
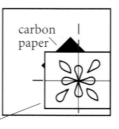
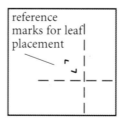

Patterns

base wood

reference grid

pattern (paper or acetate)

carbon paper

reference marks for leaf placement

Method 2 Pattern on Base

1 Photocopy the pattern to the size needed. Place acetate on pattern and trace.
2 Place acetate pattern on wood & establish reference points for placement of pattern so it will always be at same place.
3 Slip carbon paper under acetate and mark position of first inlay piece to be inlaid. Position will be transferred to wood base to guide placement of inlay piece.
4 Repeat for each inlay piece.

The Art of Wood Inlay

❧ Inlay Press ❧

Tight inlays cannot be set into a base without an inlay press. My double-screw beam style is ideal for me. If you would like the directions to make this press e-mail me at jgas@shaw.ca (see web site at www.woodinlay.ca). A ½ in threaded rod is the minimum size I would use (⅝ in rod would not be too heavy). This will provide enough clamping force to press into place inlays that are several inches square). The press must have its clamping force square to the base without tilting to the sides. A press block is required to transfer the clamping force of the press to the inlays. A press block can be any size or shape to suit your needs. The ones I use most often are made from ¾ in cedar. This soft wood is less likely to leave marks on the base wood. If the inlay pieces and base wood are fairly hard, the inlay piece will crush into the soft inlay block rather than be pushed to the bottom of the inlay cavity. To solve this problem face the inlay block with ⅛ in masonite the same size as press block. To use, stack these on top of inlay piece to be pressed into cavity. This assembly is then placed into the inlay press and the press is tightened evenly. Be sure to soften the edges of the masonite sheet so it won't mark the base when press is tightened. After each inlay, wipe the masonite block with a damp cloth to remove any glue. Clean off any glue around inlaid piece. I used a flat chisel to scrape the surface clean before sanding flush.

Scrape off excess glue with chisel or scraper

Splitting Wood

When you begin inlay work you may think that applying a heavy clamping force to the inlay pieces will cause the base to split. This rarely happens. However, try to avoid inlaying parallel to the wood grain of the base and inlaying to a depth more than half the thickness of the base. As well, splitting can occur if the base wood is checked or has a minute split that is not detected.

Note Depth of inlay cavities should be cut approximately 85 percent of the thickness of the inlay piece in order that the inlay may be pressed to the bottom of the cavity, otherwise an edge might collapse when laying one inlay on top of another. When an inlay is pressed to the bottom of the cavity and sanded smooth, the integrity of the base wood is maintained with no voids. Each new inlay is then cut into solid wood.

Completed inlay press (shown with model V175 Record woodworker's bench vise) will press inlay pieces firmly into base for tight inlays

🌿 Basic Inlay Steps 🌿

Every inlay process follows the same basic steps to put the inlaid piece in place. Use this procedure as a general guide.

1 *Select wood for inlay piece*

2 *Choose piece appropriate size for inlay*

3 *Use marking gauge for desired thickness*

4 *Cut inlay pieces at 4 corners to insure uniform thickness*

5 *Plane inlay piece for desired thickness*

6 *Transfer pattern to base and inlay pieces (p12)*

7 *Cut out traced inlay pieces in scroll saw*

8 *Sand inlay pieces to ³⁄₃₂ in to ³⁄₁₆ in thick*

9 *Sand pieces to smooth all edges*

10 *File 1° bevel on bottom edge of inlay piece*

11 *White glue inlay piece to base and scribe round it with sharp knife*

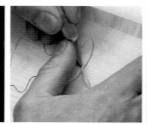

12 *Remove inlay piece and cut shoulder to scribed line*

13 *Using shoulder to back chisel, make vertical cut ¹⁄₁₆ in deeper at a time*

14 *Use curved chisels to cut rounded shapes*

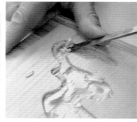

15 *Use chisels and knives to remove wood from cavity*

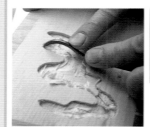

16 *Use scraping tool to smooth cavity*

17 *Use white glue to replace any small chip damage during excavating procedure*

18 *Wood filler on a toothpick fills in small gaps before pressing down inlay*

19 *Spread white carpenter's glue on all edges of inlay and cavity*

20 *Install inlay piece using press block. Pieces will not be flush (cavity should be 85% of inlay thickness)*

The Art of Wood Inlay

🌿 Making a Tight Inlay 🌿

1 File 1° angle to bottom ¹⁄₁₆ in edge of inlay piece. This is primary bevel.
2 Place inlay piece at proper location on base wood. Secure with small amount of white carpenter's glue. Hold in place a few seconds to set. Scribe around piece with sharp knife.
3 Twist off inlay piece before it has set firmly in place.
4 With scribing knife, retrace scribed line in base wood. Cut should be clean and sharp because this edge will show after the inlay is pressed into cavity.
5 Using sharp knife cut a shoulder into base wood to give a reference point to place chisel to make vertical cut.
6 Using mallet and chisel cut down ¹⁄₁₆ in at a time to chip out cavity until desired depth is reached. Cavities should be cut approximately 85% of inlay thickness.
7 Rebevel bottom edge of inlay pieces to 15°. Cover all surfaces of cavity and edges of inlay pieces with white carpenter's glue. Any edges not covered may result in small gaps at edge of inlay piece. Even under pressure glue will not flow to dry areas.
8 Place press block on top of inlay piece that is in position in inlay cavity. Place assembled unit into inlay press and press inlays into base wood until bottom of cavity is reached.
9 Remove from inlay press and clean surface of glue. Scrape glue from around inlay and sand smooth. Use 100-150 grit garnet sandpaper. Wipe glue from surface of press block with a damp cloth.

> Note It is sometimes necessary to adjust the amount of primary bevel on the inlay piece in order to accommodate the width of the scribed line or to accommodate the hardness of the wood used.

🌿 Drawing Leaves for Inlay 🌿

Nature rarely presents leaves that are flat and symmetrical. To make inlaid leaves look realistic requires thought and planning. Look at a leaf's flat side to understand the vein structure (diagram 1). To reproduce leaves with curled-up edges (diagram 2) make a mock-up leaf. Draw a single leaf on paper, cut it out, and mark the vein pattern on both sides. Fold and curl up the edges of the leaf and note the vein direction (diagram 3). Now the vein direction of the curled-up part of the leaf is visible and you can extend this idea to the inlay drawing.

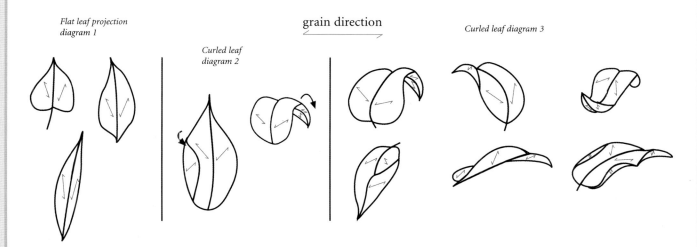

Flat leaf projection diagram 1

grain direction

Curled leaf diagram 2

Curled leaf diagram 3

🍃 Making a Leaf Construct 🍃

Leaves are generally composed of 2 pieces of wood with the wood grain simulating the vein pattern of the leaf. However the 2 pieces do not have to be inlaid separately. The pieces can be assembled into a construct and inlaid as one piece.

1 Choose wood for leaf inlay. Cut off segment needed (diagram B).
2 Cut wood segment down the center, as shown, in diagram C. This will leave each half with the grain pattern the mirror of the other. This is called book matching (diagram D).
3 Diagram D shows the 2 halves of wood pieces fitted together with matching curve cuts marked. Cut either the positive or negative side and then hand fit the opposite side. Cutting can be done with a fret saw with crow's foot. I use a scroll saw and spindle sanding drum mounted in a drill press to fit the halves together. Fitting must be done exactly so that no light shows through when the pieces are put together. Use a small file to smooth any excess wood, Glue and clamp (see diagram E).
4 Piece now must be sanded to an even thickness, usually $^3/_{16}$ in. Lay a sanding pad on work bench and pass leaf piece over it to achieve thickness.
5 Use pattern to trace desired leaf (see diagram F). Cut out (diagram G).
6 Leaf can now be inlaid as one piece.

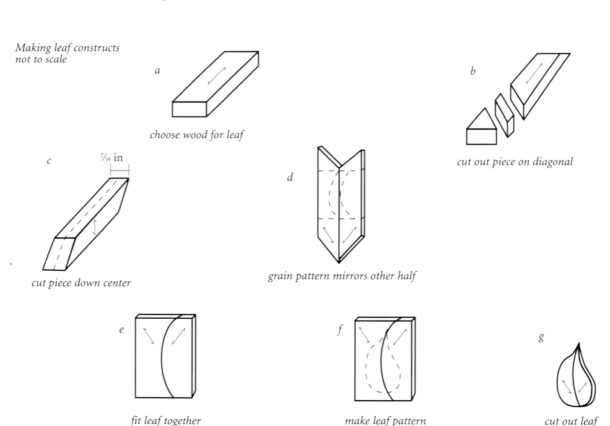

Making leaf constructs not to scale

a

choose wood for leaf

b

cut out piece on diagonal

c $^7/_{16}$ in

cut piece down center

d

grain pattern mirrors other half

e

fit leaf together matching curves

f

make leaf pattern

g

cut out leaf

🌿 Preparing Inlay Pieces 🌿

Ideally inlay pieces should be ³⁄₁₆ in thick but can range from ⅛ in to ¼ in thick. Pieces thinner than ⅛ in are difficult to inlay and not as stable when lapping of inlays is required. Pieces thicker than ¼ in require more work for no practical gain, except when inlaying end grain pieces.

Cutting Bevels

Another exception is when inlaying a large background piece that will be cut into by other inlay pieces. Thicker background inlay pieces may be desirable to help keep small pieces of background secure. Inlaying other pieces into slightly thicker background pieces is always better than cutting through the background piece.

1 When inlaying a hardwood into a hardwood do not use a primary bevel on the inlay piece unless the scribed line is very wide. This should be compensated for.

2 When inlaying a soft wood into a hard wood (or vice versa) a 1° bevel is the best place to start.

Primary Bevel

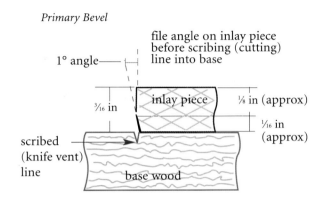

file angle on inlay piece before scribing (cutting) line into base

1° angle

³⁄₁₆ in

inlay piece

⅛ in (approx)

¹⁄₁₆ in (approx)

scribed (knife vent) line

base wood

Incorrect way to use chisel

sharp chisel

no release cut

crushed edge

scribed line cut with fine blade knife

scribed line cut with thick blade knife

Correct way to use chisel

1   **2**

chisel

scribed line   shoulder cut

shoulder cut   chisel

relief cut

chisel back to scribed line

> **Note** As a general rule use a 1° bevel on the inlay piece if the outline is cut with a knife that has a very fine blade. A thicker blade produces a wider kerf so increase the bevel slightly to accommodate this.

3 When using only soft woods a slightly greater bevel or one that tapers the thickness of inlay piece may produce the best result. If you are not sure make test inlays on scrap wood before proceeding with the project inlay.

Cutting a Vertical Edge

Driving even a very sharp chisel into a piece of wood will not produce a clean sharp edge. By making a relief cut in front of the chisel blade you are assured of a cleanly sheared and accurate cut. Diagrams show the best way to make chisel cuts.

3   **4**

chisel   shaving

clean cut edge

base wood   cavity

🌿 Inlay Techniques 🌿

1 **Constructs** Multi-piece inlays (sometimes preassembled) can provide inlay detail that would otherwise be difficult to accomplish. Constructs can be made by book matching, overlay, double inlay, two-stage inlay, and wrapped inlay.

2 **Lapped Inlay** The inlay of a piece of wood to overlap a piece already inlaid (see bulrush for basic lapping technique). Most projects require some overlap of inlays.

3 **Book Matching** If you saw a piece of wood lengthwise and spread the two halves flat, one half will be the mirror image of the other. The resulting grain pattern of the matched halves is ideal for making leaf constructs.

4 **Overlay (Inlay)** A process of forming a construct when a number of different pieces (color and/or grain) is needed to shape one figure (see rose head). The pieces can be partly assembled as constructs and inlaid in sections or the pieces can be inlaid into the base piece by piece, lapped style (see yellow rose project) or it can define the process of lapping inlay pieces or constructs in the base wood to form the picture element.

5 **Double Inlay** This process involves inlaying one inlay piece or construct into a second wood that becomes part of the final construct. After the construct has been redressed to the desired thickness and recut to its final shape, it is then inlaid as a whole into the base wood (see holly leaf and Christmas tree constructs).

6 **2-stage Inlay** This process involves forming constructs by overlaying inlay pieces into a base wood (sacrificial block) that will not become part of the final inlay construct (see candle flame construct and the bed tray flower petal construct).

7 **Wrapped Inlay** Wrap the cut out inlay piece with a thin strip of another wood to create the construct, then inlay the construct into the base wood. Used to outline or provide contrast for an inlaid piece.

8 **Shadow or Background Inlay** Used to fill in spaces between inlay pieces or constructs that require wood different from base wood (see candy dish).

9 **Primary Edge Segment** The portion of edge of the inlaid piece that will define the picture.

10 **Secondary or Minor Edge Segment** The edge segment that will be overlapped by a subsequent layer of inlay or construct (see yellow rose plaque and bed tray).

11 **Deep Inlay** Any inlaid piece or construct deeper than ¼ in (see round acorn box and deep bowl set).

12 **Scorched Edges** Use a wood burning tool to lightly char the edges of an inlay piece. Use to define inlay piece when it is the same color or grain pattern as the base piece. See photo below.

13 **End Grain** Used to create texture and depth. Note It is best to cut end grain pieces thicker to minimize cracking of inlay during pressing process. Bias cut is any end grain cut less than 90° to the face.

14 **Laminated Base** Base consists of layered wood glued together. Allow to dry 12 hours.

Decorative Butterfly Pattern (half size)

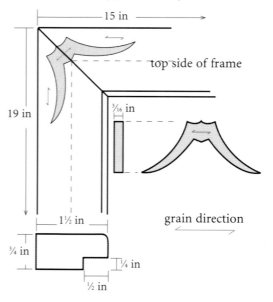

15 in

19 in

³⁄₁₆ in

top side of frame

1½ in

¾ in

¼ in

½ in

grain direction

Picture Frame

Using the inlay techniques described on pp14,15 butterflies can be installed easily on any project without investing in expensive tools. Butterflies can act as structural support for a wood joint or can be added decoration or both. An example is a butterfly used to make a picture frame. The use of contrasting or the same woods, such as white birch or cherry in a cherry frame can add a decorative touch.

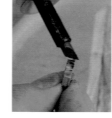

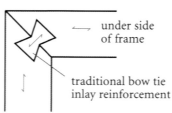

under side of frame

traditional bow tie inlay reinforcement

🌿 Repairing Inlay 🌿

Sometimes a piece of wood is chipped off the side of the inlay cavity. It can be repaired easily leaving no trace of the flaw.

Shows flaw to be repaired

A wedge of wood is made to inlay in flaw, matching grain

Base is excavated to inlay repair piece

Repair piece is pressed into place before sanding

Repair piece sanded flush

Being able to inlay one piece of wood into another consistently and with great precision is useful for other wood repair and to reinforce wood joints. This patch technique is called a Dutchman.

It can be applied to a board to repair an elongated knothole or an area of shallow rot in an otherwise sound board. For example, an elongated diamond shape hole aligned with the grain can be fitted with a patch cut to fit tightly into the hole. Glued in with epoxy, this repair will make the plank as strong or stronger than one cut unblemished from virgin timber. To fix an area of rot, make the patch first. Lay out a symmetrical elongated diamond on a piece of scrap wood, scribe around the patch and carve out the shape with a router or hand chisel. Glue the patch in the cavity with epoxy. This will result in a strong water-tight repair. Sand or plane smooth when dry. To repair a damaged surface such as a table top the shape can be any one you choose. If a very close grain match can be found for the patch, it is possible to effect a repair to the surface that is almost undetectable.

Another kind of patch traditionally used by Hawaiians to repair food or storage bowls is called a Flying Dutchman. Cracks in bark, imperfections, or sap pockets can be repaired in this way. This "butterfly" or "bow tie" wood patch provides great strength. It can also be used to reinforce wood joints. Inlay the butterfly across the wood joint, glue in place, sand, and finish as required. The design of the butterfly and the choice of wood can be plain or decorative.

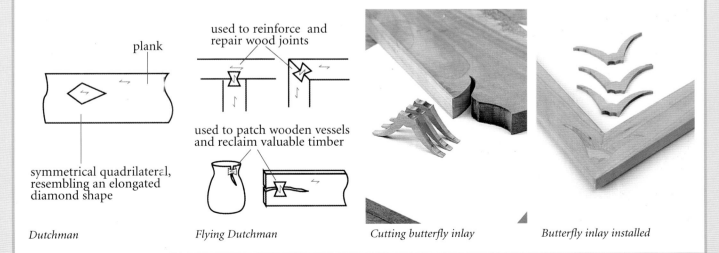

plank

symmetrical quadrilateral, resembling an elongated diamond shape

Dutchman

used to reinforce and repair wood joints

used to patch wooden vessels and reclaim valuable timber

Flying Dutchman

Cutting butterfly inlay

Butterfly inlay installed

🍃 Finishing 🍃

Jamie Almond

Proper finishing of inlay pieces is very important. It enhances the look of the project. It's true to say that inlay does not reach its full visual potential until the top coat goes on. To achieve the best result requires patience and testing. Try out various finishes such as lacquer, acrylic, urethane, or oil on a piece of the same wood as the project until you get the effect you want. It's easier to do this than to refinish the piece later because the results are not suitable. It's also important to know characteristics of the wood you are finishing. Whether the wood is open or closed grain or naturally oily (see chart on p126) affects the kind of finish that needs to be applied as well as the way it is applied. The way the wood is cut (see chart on p127) will also affect how the finish will look.

Flat surface sanding, rub object on sandpaper surface

Wood block has shaped surfaces to cover with sandpaper for contour sanding

Finishing Problems

Several problems that can affect the finish may not be readily apparent until the first finishing coat is applied. If you look for these beforehand you will save yourself unnecessary work and disappointment. The following are the most common.

1 **Unseen Scratches** Open grain woods or closed grain such as oak or mahogany often have scratches that are difficult to see. Different wood types and cuts used in a single inlay design often make traditional sanding of the piece a problem so other methods are needed to deal with scratches. Scraping with the back of a well sharpened chisel or a cabinet maker's scraping blade is the best way to deal with this problem. Sanding scratches is also possible if you approach the process with great care. Begin with an orbital sander and 100 grit sandpaper and sand entire area evenly until the scratch is not visible, then use 120 or 150 grit and move to 220 grit. After the sanding is completed scrape the inlay before applying the finish.

Using a Scraping Tool

1 Scraper must be kept sharp, especially using it for inlay where it is not always used with the grain of the wood. Softer woods can tear or be gouged but a sharp scraper will take off perfect little shavings and leave a glass-like surface which will be much better than a sanded surface.

2 If the scraper creates only dust it is time to reestablish the burr/hook (you can do this 3 to 4 times between sharpenings) or resharpen. This may vary depending on the wood you are scraping.

3 Scraper should sharpen to approximately 5° angle for fine work such as inlay and close to a 10° angle for paint or layers removal.

4 When burnishing the edge you can use practically any steel rod (the shank of a screwdriver). However, a burnishing tool produces better results.

5 Test the scraper on scrap wood after sharpening to check the edge. If it is incorrectly sharpened it can be worse than sanding scratches.

Use a 1 in chisel and cabinet scrapers for scraping. Hold the scraping tool in both hands and apply pressure with thumbs on center of tool for forward motion and with fingers to draw back to body

2 Bleeding Some exotic woods such as padauk or pao rosa have a high oil content and when sanded could bleed their natural wood color into surrounding inlay pieces. To prevent this from happening wipe in one direction (do not rub) the inlay piece with ethyl alcohol a minimum of two hours before applying a sealer. When the alcohol has dissipated check visually to see if the wood is emitting any more oil or lay on paper towel. If so, repeat the alcohol application. Another way to eliminate this problem is to precut the wood piece you are going to use in the inlay to the desired thickness and allow it to air dry, allowing the oils to dissipate naturally. Drying can take a month or more. Only epoxy resins can contain tree sap and these are expensive and have a strong odor. NGR (non grain raising) finishes or precatalyzed lacquer or acrylic finishes will mitigate the problem, but these are very expensive and require some expertise and equipment to use.

3 Glue A tiny amount of glue left on the inlay surface can spoil the finish. To make sure no glue remains check the project under different lighting (I use natural, incandescent, and fluorescent). Scraping removes glue very well and also provides a scratch-free surface.

4 Uneven Finishes Because the inlay design is made from various cuts and types of wood which react to the finish differently, the finished surface may appear uneven. End grain, edge grain, and surface grain as well as flat cut, quarter cut, rotary cut, and rift cut all absorb a finish in different ways. Testing is the best way to find out how the different cuts of woods react to the finish. Use a piece of wood the same as the inlay piece and apply a finish to a small portion. Allow to dry, then cover this with a piece of cardboard and apply another finish to another part of the wood. Repeat this for all the finishes

Set project on wood blocks to spray bottom edge and to dry

Jamie Almond applying spray finish to a project. He wears a quality mask and sprays by a filtered exhaust system that fits into window and removes harmful vapor to outside

you might use. You can also try the same finishes but in different sheens (flat, satin, semi gloss, gloss). You should also apply a sealer coat and then apply the finishes. A sealer coat on oak, for example, will even out the finish. Sometimes an uneven finish or texture is desirable on the inlay project because it can add depth and character. Your choice of finish depends on the effect you wish to create. However, an uneven finish that resembles fish eyes or orange peel is not desirable. Many things can cause these undesirable effects.

- Oil on the wood surface from the wood or your hands. Best to wear gloves when handling the unfinished wood inlay project. Wipe the wood with alcohol to remove (oil on oily woods).
- Wax on the wood surface. Wipe with alcohol on a lint-free cloth or cheesecloth, then scrape or sand.
- Insufficient drying time between coats. Allow coat to dry thoroughly, then scrape and sand the finish off and start again.
- Poor ambient temperature or humidity in the work area of finish being used is too hot or too cold will affect the application of the finish.

5 Bloom Sprayed finishes need sufficient drying time between coats, otherwise a milky-white cloudy look appears. When this happens stop spraying and allow coat to dry thoroughly before proceeding.

6 Uneven Surface Sanding or scraping may cause a low spot on the surface which is not noticed until the first finish coat is applied. This is more noticeable with gloss or semi-gloss, lacquer, urethane, or acrylic which reflect light than with an oil finish which absorbs light. Try to scrape or sand uneven surface or layer the surface by applying the finish in a light coat or multiple coats to build up the low area, then apply the finish to entire inlay. Repeat if necessary. Allow to dry between coats and sand with 150 or 220 grit sandpaper. Remove dust with a vacuum or tack cloth. Do not try to even out the low spot all at once because the finish in the low spot will be thicker than the surrounding finish and you may create a high spot.

Finish Types

Inlay projects require special care in finishing. I have tried many different finishes and these are the ones I recommend.

1 **Oil** (any kind can be used but Danish and Antique Oil Finish are my favorites) is easy to apply with a lint-free cloth or foam brush. It is inexpensive and available at any home improvement store. It cleans up with soap and water. However, oil can vary the color on inlay depending on the wood used and it offers minimal UV protection against fading of wood color.
2 **Urethane/Varathane** (I prefer Flecto and Behr) is easy to apply using spray or foam brush. It is inexpensive, fast drying, forms a hard protective finish, and offers better UV protection. However, this finish can run and gives a heavier look. It is highly volatile and has a strong odor so must be applied outdoors or in a well ventilated area or spray booth with a ventilation system.
3 **Lacquer** is my finish of choice because it is easy to apply using spray or foam brush, is fast drying, and provides a hard protective finish that is natural looking. It has the widest range of non reactive issues with exotic woods and offers better UV protection. However, this finish is more expensive than oils or urethanes, has the potential for runs, and is highly volatile. Because of the strong odor the finish must be applied outdoors or in a well ventilated area or spray booth with a ventilation system.

Safety

In addition to the safe handling of power tools and sharp chisels when doing wood inlay, observe the same caution when using finishing materials.
1 Observe all the warning precautions listed on the material label and follow the manufacturer's directions for the material's use.
2 Wear vented goggles or safety glasses.
3 Wear a dust mask or respirator that is approved for the finish you select.
4 Spray finishes in a ventilated area or spray booth with filtered exhaust system.
5 Wear disposable latex gloves, painter's disposable suit to protect skin.
6 Have patience and take the time to follow all the recommended steps.

Portable 2-stage exhaust system has solids filter and charcoal filter for fumes

Finishing Procedures

The time spent on the preparation of the wood inlay project prior to applying the finish will ensure the best results. All pieces in this book were finished by hand and aerosol can spray. Expensive finishing equipment is not needed to achieve a professional look. Follow these steps for successful finishing.
1 Check the project carefully under different lighting (indoor lighting and sunlight) for scratches.
2 A scratch that is not too deep can be scraped out; if it is deeper, sand and then scrape.
3 Vacuum off the dust and also wipe with a tack cloth if necessary.
4 Look at the kinds of woods that are used in the inlay and decide on an appropriate finish for texture or character.
5 Apply the finish according to the manufacturer's instructions using a foam brush or spray (keep 6 in to 8 in away from the project). Allow drying time according to the manufacturer's recommendation. Sand with 220 grit sandpaper between coats and vacuum off the dust before applying the next coat.
6 Apply a minimum of 1 sealer and 2 top coats on all surfaces. This is usually sufficient to seal the project to prevent uneven shrinkage and future cracking of wood. Additional coats depend on your artist's eye and how you want the project to look.

Napkin Holder

T

This simple but attractive project can be made from pieces of wood left over from other projects

Base Material
Aspen 16 in x 9 in x ⅜ in thick
Inlay Material
Black poplar

Base Construction
Use dimensions for napkin holder given on pattern opposite. I used a fine tooth handsaw to cut sides of the napkin holder and finished the edges on the disk sander. Using a power tool on this wood will cause chipping and tearing of the edges.

Inlay Procedure
1 Transfer (p12) inlay pattern pieces (p25) onto black poplar and cut out.
2 Use pattern to position each inlay piece on base material in order given on p25. To make leaf constructs see p16. Follow directions for inlay procedure on p14.

Note Project uses lap inlay, book match, & constructs techniques

Inlays cut from scrap black poplar

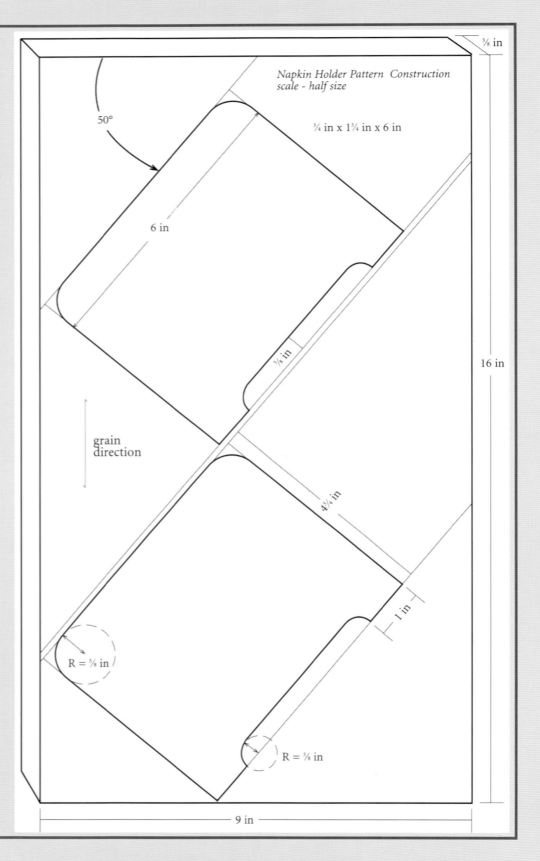

Napkin Holder Pattern Construction scale - half size

¾ in x 1¼ in x 6 in

50°

6 in

grain direction

⅜ in

4¾ in

R = ⅝ in

1 in

R = ⅜ in

⅜ in

16 in

9 in

Napkin Holder Inlay Pattern
Side A   scale - half size

grain
direction

Napkin Holder Inlay Pattern
Side B   scale - half size

Napkin Holder -wood choices & steps
not to scale

Aspen (base wood)
Black poplar (flat grain)
Black poplar (flat grain)
Black poplar (end grain for floral center)

Side A

Side B

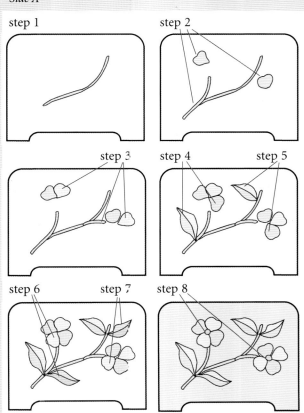

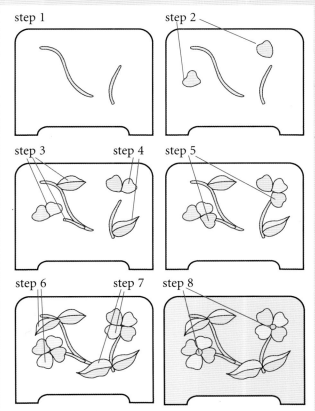

Napkin holder

Vegetable Wall Plaque

The color and grain pattern in different woods often suggest what can be made of the wood piece. That is how I chose the inlay wood for the vegetables in this plaque.

Base Material

Maple 16 in x 6 in planed to ½ in thickness American cherry ¼ in x ⅝ in strips

Inlay Material

Russian olive, sandpaper wood, holly, tulip poplar, padauk, pernambuco, purpleheart, black poplar in various small pieces

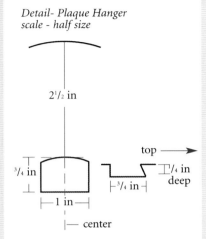

Detail- Plaque Hanger
scale - half size

2½ in

top →

¾ in

¼ in deep

¾ in

1 in

center

Note   Project uses lap inlay, constructs, & scorching techniques

Base Construction

Make plaque from hard maple. See diagram. I made a frame for this piece from ¼ in x ⅝ in strip of American cherry. Make the hanging slot as shown.

Inlay Procedure

1 Transfer pattern (p12) for inlay pieces onto inlay material and cut out. Arrange pattern inlay pieces on base and inlay them. Follow directions for inlay procedure on p14.
2 Cut out each section of large mushroom from a different part of Russian olive. Inlay stem first and then lap mushroom cap over end of stem.
3 Cut out complete shape of small mushrooms from sandpaper wood. Cut off stems and scorch cut areas to define piece. Inlay each piece separately or make construct (p16) and inlay construct.
4 For green onions glue a piece of poplar to a piece of holly. Dry. Cut out onion pattern. Form the green onion pieces from scraps of tulip poplar, using the construct method. Inlay underlying extra green piece first. Then inlay the green onion construct on top of the first piece.
5 Cut beet pieces from purpleheart, large carrots from padauk, small carrots from pernambuco. Inlay each as single piece.

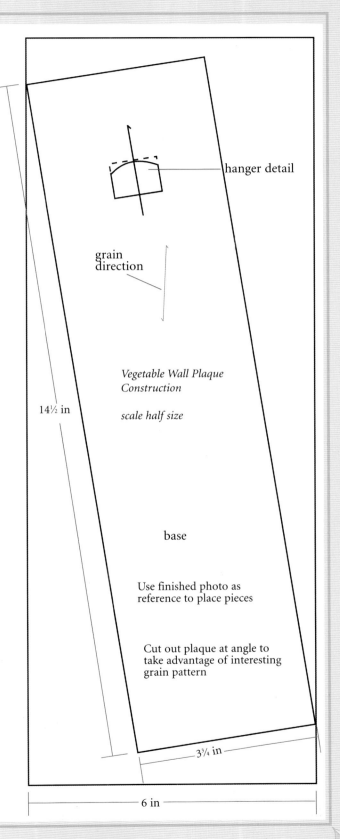

hanger detail

grain direction

Vegetable Wall Plaque Construction

scale half size

14½ in

base

Use finished photo as reference to place pieces

Cut out plaque at angle to take advantage of interesting grain pattern

3¾ in

6 in

Vegetable Wall Plaque- Patterns
scale - half size

grain
direction

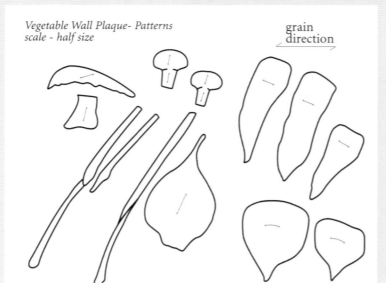

Make large mushroom stem
& cap from Russian olive

Make small mushrooms
from sandpaper wood

Make onion from black
poplar

Make large carrot from
padauk

Wood choices
scale - half size

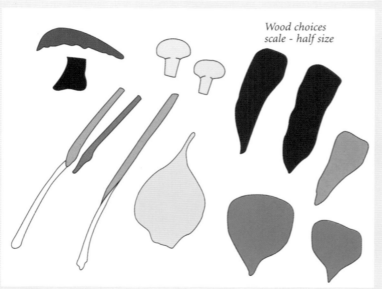

Make small carrot from
pernambuco

Make beets from purpleheart
Cut from large knot giving
round perspective to inlay
piece

▬	Purpleheart
▬	Tulip poplar
▬	Tulip poplar (different shade)
▬	Padauk
▬	Russian olive
▬	Russian olive (same piece)
▬	Pernambuco
▬	Sandpaper wood
▬	Black poplar
▬	Holly wood

Detail - Frame corner construction
scale - half size

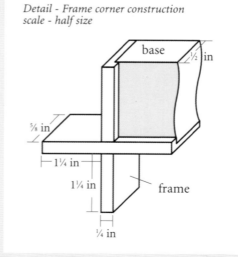

base
½ in

⅝ in

1¼ in

1¼ in

frame

¼ in

Mushroom Paddle Trivet

Woods suggested here are my choice but other woods may be substituted. Wood color and grain patterns can be effective in the inlay design.

Base Material
Maple planed to 1 in thickness
Inlay Material
Siberian elm, Honduras mahogany, tulip poplar, Philippine mahogany (end grain cut)

Trivet Construction
Make trivet according to diagram from maple 1 in thick. Finish all edges with ⅛ in round over router bit. Make ⅝ in hole in trivet handle and finish hole edges with ⅛ in round over router bit.

Inlay Procedure
1 Transfer pattern (p12) for inlay pieces onto inlay material and cut out. Use the pattern to position each inlay piece on base material. Follow directions for inlay procedure on p14.
2 Follow step numbers on diagram for suggested order of inlay.

Note Project uses lap inlay technique

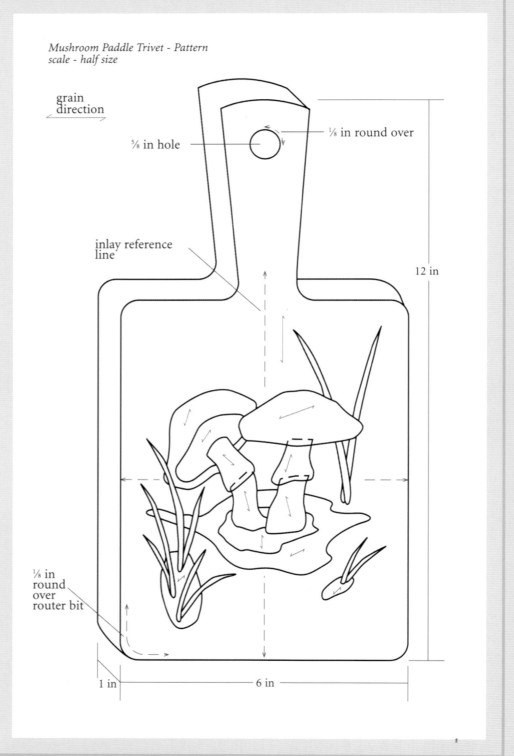

Mushroom Paddle Trivet - Pattern scale - half size

grain direction

⅝ in hole

⅛ in round over

inlay reference line

12 in

⅛ in round over router bit

1 in

6 in

The Art of Wood Inlay

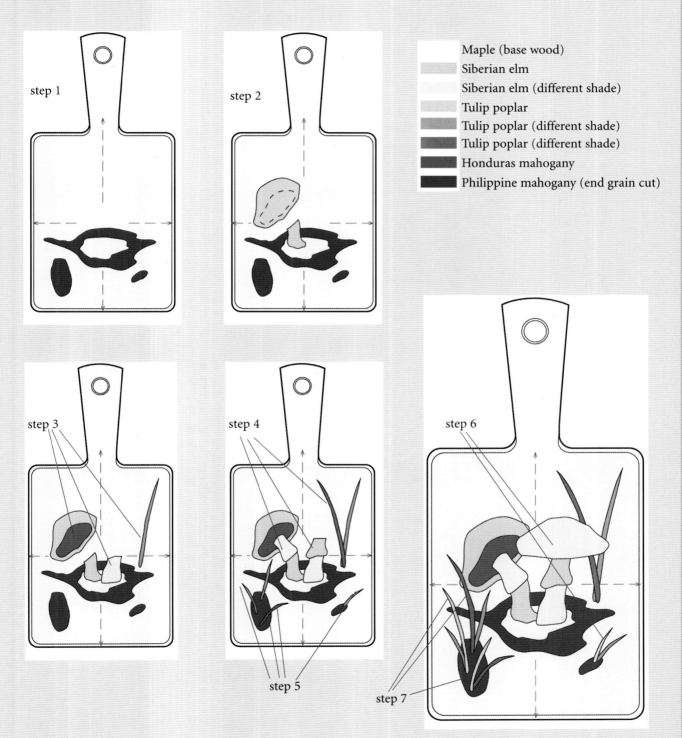

Wood choices & steps
not to scale

step 1

step 2

Maple (base wood)
Siberian elm
Siberian elm (different shade)
Tulip poplar
Tulip poplar (different shade)
Tulip poplar (different shade)
Honduras mahogany
Philippine mahogany (end grain cut)

step 3

step 4

step 6

step 5

step 7

Bulrush Plaques 1 & 2

Plaque 2

Plaque 1

Decorative plaques take advantage of knotty pine and yellow pine to make unusual frame.

Bulrush Plaque 1

Base Material
Knotty pine 1 in x 8 in x 12 in
Yellow pine 1 in x 6 in x 16 in

Inlay Material
Western red cedar, oak, mahogany, redwood, gumwood

Plaque Construction

1 Shape plaque base from knotty pine according to measurements.
2 Cut yellow pine into 1 in strips 2 ½ in long. Angle ends to 10°.
3 Arrange pieces for most attractive variation of grain and color.
4 Glue edges together (10 wide) with ends evenly aligned.
5 Rabbet both sides of the base wood ⅜ in x ⅜ in on the face side. Make equal size rabbets on the end of the yellow pine pieces that are glued together. Glue onto side of base.
6 Trim to ½ in width. Repeat on the other side.
7 Rabbet ends of plaque base and glue on pieces of yellow pine wiht the ⅜ in rabbet cut along the grain of the yellow pine and trim to ½ in width. See diagram below.

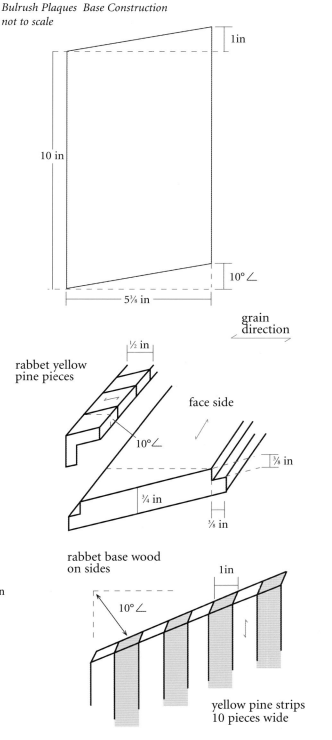

Bulrush Plaques Base Construction not to scale

1 in

10 in

10° ∠

5⅜ in

grain direction

rabbet yellow pine pieces

½ in

10° ∠

face side

¾ in

⅜ in

⅜ in

rabbet base wood on sides

1 in

10° ∠

yellow pine strips 10 pieces wide

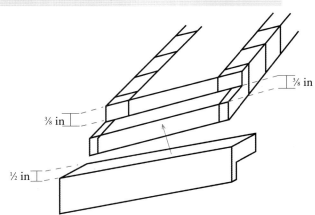

⅜ in

⅜ in

½ in

Inlay Procedure

1 Choose oak for water ripple and 3 shades of cedar.

2 Make inlay pieces (p14) from pattern and cut out. Use #2 X-acto knife to scribe lines around inlay pieces and make vertical cuts in base with ⅛ in chisel and mallet.

3 Follow inlay procedure steps on p14.

4 Use 2 different end grain cuts of mahogany for bulrush heads for different textures. To inlay end grain cuts, cut them a bit thicker (¼ in if possible). Pressing in end grain pieces sometimes causes them to crack under pressure if the clamping force is not exactly even. Thicker pieces do not do this. Bulrush leaves in this project are long and slender and actually strengthen the base. Each leaf as it is inlaid will help keep the base from cracking.

5 I chose oak for the water ripple because the grain suggests ripples of water. Cut the oak ripple on jigsaw on slight angle to give depth perception (See diagram on p36). The water ripple is the largest single inlay in this project and should be inlaid slightly deeper that the other pieces to give more stability when inlaying bulrush leaves. Be sure water ripple is evenly seated in the inlay cavity, otherwise hollow spaces may allow an edge to collapse when leaves are pressed into ripple. When inlaying more than 2 pieces close together allow each inlay piece to set until glue dries completely (see E on p36). Set larger underlying pieces deeper so pieces that overlay it will cut into it and not through it. Fill in uneven surfaces on the bottom of inlay cavity with wood filler. Then apply glue to all surfaces and press inlay into place before filler has set.

6 I chose Western red cedar for the leaves because of its variety of shades. Transfer leaf patterns to cedar (p12) and cut out. Prepare to inlay (p14).

Wood choices

Plane thickness to make ³⁄₁₆ in oak slice for water ripple

Transfer pattern for inlay pieces (p12)

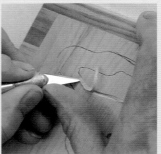

Inlay water ripple first and deeper to provide stability for bulrush leaves. Cut vertical at ends of bulrush leaves with ⅛ in curved round chisel

> **Note** The knot in the wood behind the bulrush leaf adds to the scene as the rising sun. Plan to take advantage of any wood color or grain variations to enhance your project.

Marking desired thickness of inlay piece

Cut inlay piece to proper thickness starting at 4 corners so cut is even.

Cutting inlay piece on scroll saw

Water ripple inlay

7 Redwood was chosen for the stems and gumwood for the spikes on the bulrush heads. Treat each element differently by your choice of wood grain and shade.

8 Use green tulip poplar (natural color of wood) for the short grass. Note This green color will change to brown over time when exposed to ultraviolet light but this will not detract from the beauty of the piece.

9 When you inlay the light cedar leaf on the right side of picture a small sliver of water ripple will remain (see D on p36) between it and adjacent leaf. Allow this area to set completely while you proceed with inlay of bulrush heads. When inlaying leaf piece be sure knife is very sharp to make a clean shoulder cut on which the chisel will rest. Gently cut down vertical edge ¹⁄₁₆ in at a time. Making a relief cut down the center of leaf will allow the wood chips to break to the center, relieving the stress on the sliver of water ripple. Watch for any small chips that might beak loose and reglue into place. Note If you carve this edge with knife only there will be less stress and provide a better result.

10 When lapping one inlay over or through another, usually you do not have to wait for the underlying inlay to set completely.

11 Make inlay piece. Cut out bulrush head space in base. Press in place.

12 As each piece is inlaid, immediately scrape off all traces of glue expelled from cavity. Then sand surface of base wood to remove all traces of glue.

Note Project uses lap inlay technique

Cutting verticals of cavity for bulrush leaves with ⅛ in straight chisel

Removing inlay after scribing is completed

Use disk sander and spindle sander on drill press to shape oak ripple

Use a crow's foot and small half round wood file to put bevel on oak ripple inlay piece

Note Small nicks in the edge of inlay cavity or on places where the edge has been excessively undercut should be repaired before inlay is pressed in place. Place a small amount of wood filler in the cavity next to the flaw. Do not allow to set. Apply glue as usual in cavity and on inlay piece, then quickly press into place. Use enough glue on all edges of inlay piece and cavity to completely lubricate them. Do not leave any dry spots which may leave a small hole in the surface which will be difficult to repair.

Cut into marked lines for water ripple with chisel and mallet

Inlaying bulrush head with curved chisel

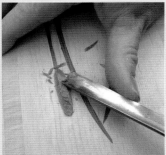

Using curved gouge to help trim inlay flush

Finding flat grain is not always on top side of wood

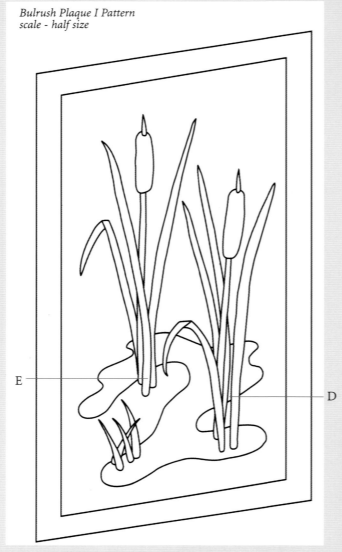

Bulrush Plaque I Pattern
scale - half size

E

D

Inlay water ripple first. Cut water ripple from oak sheet angled to one side to create depth

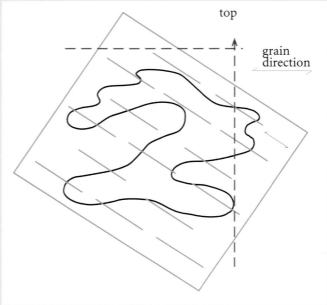

top

grain direction

Bulrush head

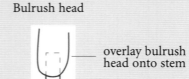

overlay bulrush head onto stem

inlay stem

Leaf inlay

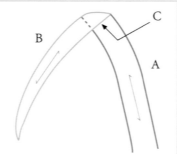

B

C

A

Inlay A first
Overlay B on top of A to leave clean joint at C

The Art of Wood Inlay

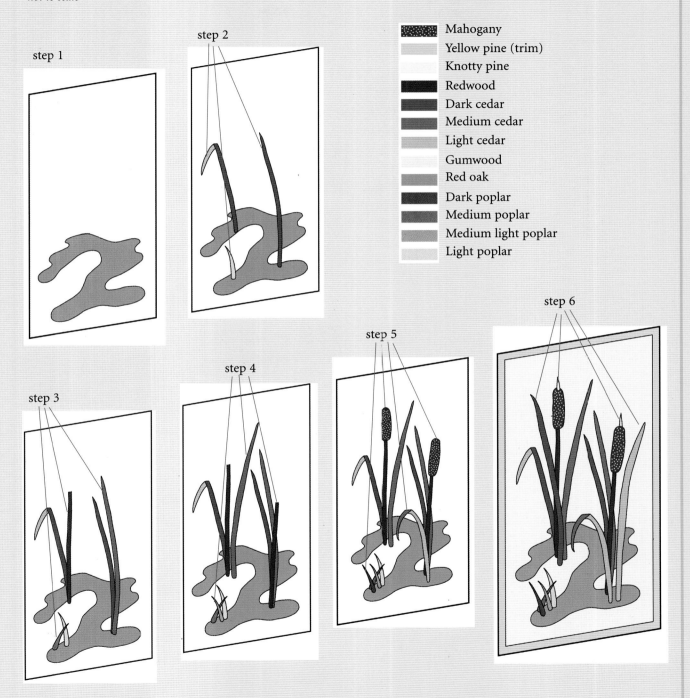

Bulrush 1 - wood choices & steps
not to scale

step 1

step 2

Mahogany
Yellow pine (trim)
Knotty pine
Redwood
Dark cedar
Medium cedar
Light cedar
Gumwood
Red oak
Dark poplar
Medium poplar
Medium light poplar
Light poplar

step 3

step 4

step 5

step 6

Bulrush Plaque 2

The materials used, construction procedures, and
inlay techniques are the same as Bulrush 1

Bulrush Plaque 2 Pattern
scale - half size

Bulrush 2 - wood choices & steps
not to scale

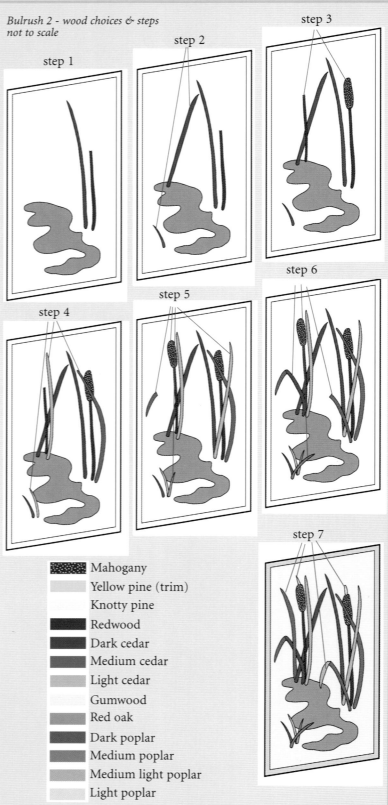

step 1

step 2

step 3

step 4

step 5

step 6

step 7

	Mahogany
	Yellow pine (trim)
	Knotty pine
	Redwood
	Dark cedar
	Medium cedar
	Light cedar
	Gumwood
	Red oak
	Dark poplar
	Medium poplar
	Medium light poplar
	Light poplar

Decorative Tiles

I made the inlay pieces for these tiles from wood scraps left over from other projects. I keep these small pieces stored in pails sorted in species of wood.

Base Material
American cherry, hard maple, elm, red oak

Inlay Material
Purpleheart, (grapes) tulip poplar (leaves, stem)

Pao rosa (cherries), tulip poplar (leaves), Russian olive (branch)

Caragana (daffodil flower petals), tulip poplar (leaves, stem)

Wenge (tree branch), tulip poplar (leaves), Manitoba maple (blossom petals), mahogany (blossom centers)

Base Construction
Make the base according to the pattern instructions given. Make 4 tiles.

Inlay Procedure

1 Grapes
Transfer (p12) pattern for inlay pieces onto inlay material. Cut out. Using reference grid lines, inlay one piece at a time using lapping technique. Follow inlay procedure steps (p14).

2 Cherries
Transfer (p12) pattern for inlay pieces onto inlay material. Cut out. Using reference grid lines, inlay one piece at a time using lapping technique. Follow inlay procedure steps (p14).

3 Daffodil
Transfer (p12) pattern for inlay pieces onto inlay material. Cut out. Using reference grid lines, inlay one piece at a time using lapping technique. Use flat cutting or rift cutting (across the grain) to make miniature timbers, planks, or boards from caragana bush twigs. Cut daffodil pieces from the center of these small planks. Follow inlay procedure steps (p14).

4 Tree Blossoms
Transfer (p12) pattern for inlay pieces onto inlay material. Cut out. Using reference grid lines, inlay one piece at a time using lapping technique. Follow inlay procedure steps (p14).

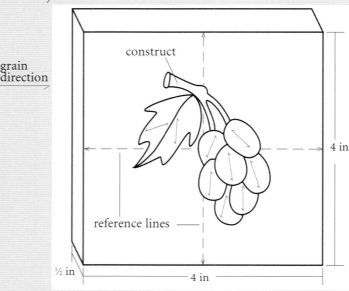

Grapes Tile Pattern
scale - half size

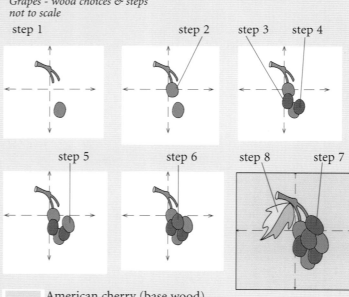

Grapes - wood choices & steps
not to scale

	American cherry (base wood)
	Purpleheart
	Purpleheart (different shade)
	Purpleheart (different shade)
	Tulip poplar
	Tulip poplar (different shade)
	Tulip poplar (different shade)

Cherries Tile Pattern
scale - half size

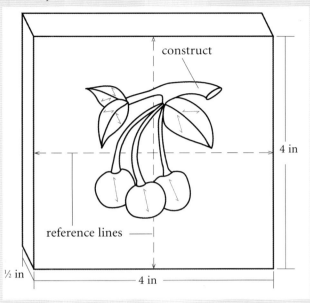

construct

reference lines

grain direction

4 in

½ in
4 in

Daffodil Tile Pattern
scale - half size

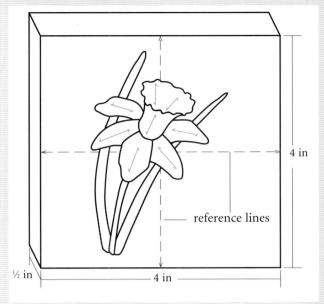

reference lines

4 in

½ in
4 in

Cherries - wood choices & steps
not to scale

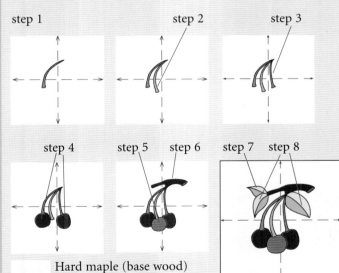

step 1   step 2   step 3

step 4   step 5   step 6   step 7   step 8

Hard maple (base wood)
Pao rosa
Pao rosa (different shade)
Pao rosa (different shade)
Tulip poplar
Tulip poplar (different shade)
Tulip poplar (different shade)
Russian olive
Russian olive (end grain cut)

Daffodil -wood choices & steps
not to scale

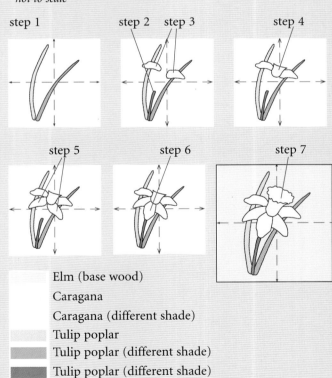

step 1   step 2   step 3   step 4

step 5   step 6   step 7

Elm (base wood)
Caragana
Caragana (different shade)
Tulip poplar
Tulip poplar (different shade)
Tulip poplar (different shade)

Note Project uses constructs, book match, & lap inlay techniques

Tree Blossoms Pattern
scale - full size

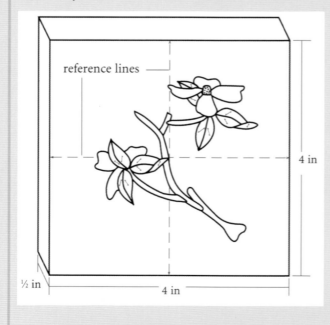

grain
direction

Tree Blossoms Tile Pattern
scale - half size

reference lines

4 in

½ in

4 in

Tree Blossoms - wood choices & steps
not to scale

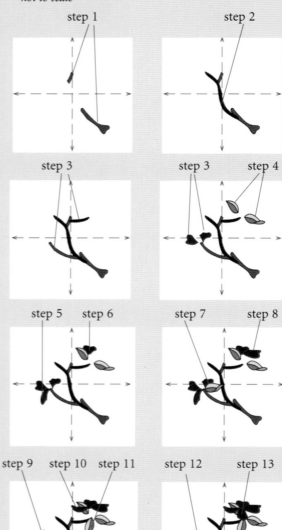

step 1

step 2

step 3

step 3   step 4

step 5   step 6   step 7   step 8

step 9   step 10   step 11   step 12   step 13

step 14

███	Manitoba maple
███	Wenge
███	Wenge (different part of same wood)
░░░	Tulip poplar
▓▓▓	Tulip poplar (different shade)
▓▓▓	Tulip poplar (different shade)
███	Mahogany
▓▓▓	Red oak (base wood)

The Art of Wood Inlay

Candy Dish

This ornamental hexagon dish is an example of background inlay where the background strips are inlaid first. Inlay procedure is basic lapping technique.

Base Material
Red oak $^{13}/_{16}$ in x approx. 9 in
Inlay Material
Black walnut, osage orange, padauk

Base Construction

1 Use pieces of $^{13}/_{16}$ in red oak glued together to obtain proper width (approx. 9 in).
2 Hexagon router pattern is marked out on a circle 14½ in diameter.
3 Mark and cut out pattern from 1/2 in plywood or other suitable pattern material.
4 Secure to base wood and filler blocks with small nails (see diagram C).
5 Diagram C detail B shows a router base of 7 in diameter. To establish inside dimension of dish use ¾ in core box router bit (detail C).
6 Cut down to a depth of ½ in during several stages (diagram D, detail E).
7 Make router base larger in diameter by ½ in to make a second cut using a ½ in straight cut router bit to begin to carve out center of dish (diagram C, details D & E).
8 Continue to carve out all remaining material of dish (diagram C, detail F). Carve down ½ in by several stages (diagram D, detail D). Then mark outside dimensions of dish (diagram C, detail G).
9 I cut oversize ⅛ in to achieve a sharp top edge after sanding to proper size on disk sander (diagram D, detail B).
10 Round over outside bottom edge with ½ in round over router bit (diagram D, detail A).
11 Diagram D, detail C shows that inlays were carved into bottom to a depth of ⅛ in.

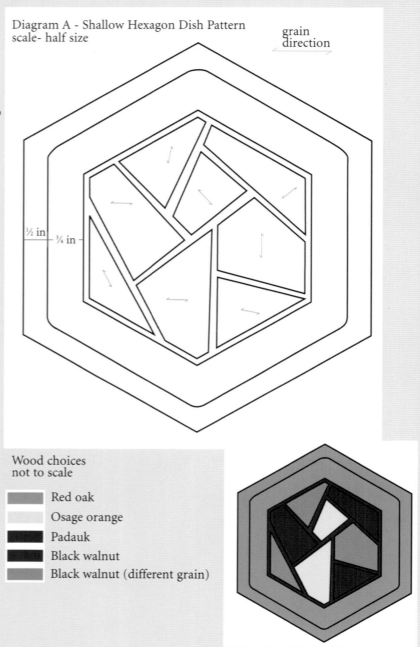

Diagram A - Shallow Hexagon Dish Pattern
scale- half size

grain direction

½ in — ¾ in

Wood choices
not to scale

▨	Red oak
▨	Osage orange
▨	Padauk
▨	Black walnut
▨	Black walnut (different grain)

Inlay Procedure

1 Background inlay is overlaid with simple pattern shapes. Background inlay provides border strips around inlaid shapes and around perimeter of design.
2 See diagram B for order to inlay background, then inlay shapes.

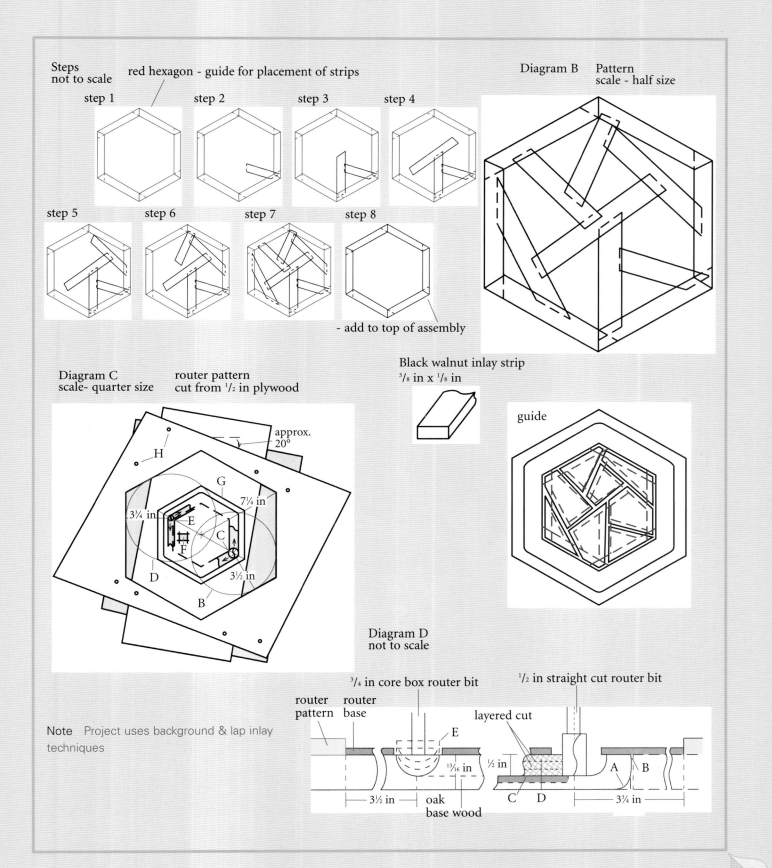

Steps
not to scale

red hexagon - guide for placement of strips

step 1 step 2 step 3 step 4

step 5 step 6 step 7 step 8

- add to top of assembly

Diagram B   Pattern
scale - half size

Diagram C
scale- quarter size

router pattern
cut from ¹/₂ in plywood

Black walnut inlay strip
³/₈ in x ¹/₈ in

guide

H

approx.
20°

G

7¼ in

3¾ in

E

C

F

B

D

3½ in

Diagram D
not to scale

Note   Project uses background & lap inlay
techniques

³/₄ in core box router bit

¹/₂ in straight cut router bit

router
pattern

router
base

layered cut

E

13/16 in

½ in

A   B

C   D

3½ in   oak
base wood

3¾ in

Poinsettia Plaque

This pattern was made from a greeting card that I liked. There are many pieces to the inlay but they can be inlaid as constructs so the inlay procedure is not too difficult. Enlarge the pattern on the photocopy machine.

Base Material
Elm 11 in x 16 in x 1¼ in
Inlay Material
Tulip poplar, pao rosa, amarillo

Base Construction

1 Draw base pattern on lightweight cardboard according to measurements on diagram 1. To establish 2 pivot points draw an arc with a compass (points C & D) on the center line. The length of the arch C & D is equal to half the length of the base, or equal to points A & B. Drive 2 small nails into the pattern at the pivot points. Tie a piece of string to form a loop equal in length to the distance between points C & E. Place string loop around both pivot points. Place a pencil inside string loop and on point E. Move pencil left or right to draw oval shape of desired dimension.

2 Cut out cardboard pattern. Tilt oval pattern 25° from center line on base wood to provide interesting background for inlay. Trace around pattern. Cut out.

Inlay Procedure

1 Establish inlay reference lines on base wood oval to position poinsettia pattern. Continue to use these reference lines for accurate position of each inlay element.

2 Using diagram for leaves and stems (p48) make a pattern using carbon paper for each stem and leaf. Cut out. This will be the pattern for the constructs. Diagram shows numbered order to do inlays.

3 Leaf number 1 combines 2 inlay techniques. The top half of the leaf is a construct of 2 assembled pieces (A). The third element of the leaf is overlaid as a separate piece (B).

4 Poinsettia flower involves inlaying 3 separate layers of petal constructs (see p49). Petals are numbered in order of inlay. Also number each petal construct so you can identify its position.

5 Inlay each element of flower center. Make first release cut with a drill bit slightly smaller than inlay pieces. Use ¹⁄₁₆ in chisel to trim back to scribed line. Taper each piece slightly to fit hole tightly when pressed in place.

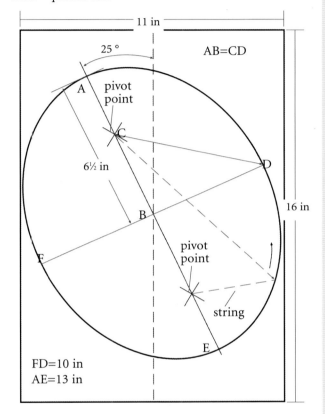

Diagram 1- Base construction
scale - quarter size

11 in

25 °

AB=CD

A

pivot point

C

6½ in

D

B

16 in

F

pivot point

string

E

FD=10 in
AE=13 in

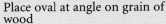

Place oval at angle on grain of wood

Trace pattern pieces

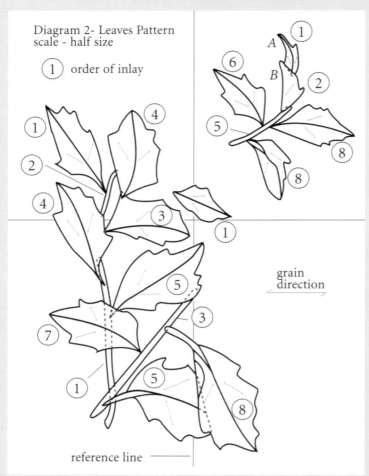

Diagram 2- Leaves Pattern
scale - half size

(1) order of inlay

A
B

grain direction

reference line

Leaves choices & steps
not to scale

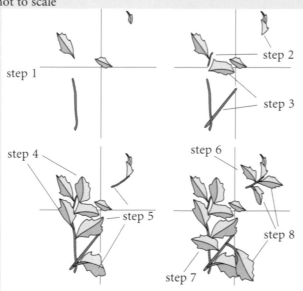

step 1
step 2
step 3
step 4
step 5
step 6
step 7
step 8

Shape of petal

Petal is book matched (p17)

Trace pattern onto book matched inlay material

Pattern is traced on inlay wood

Cut out petal shape with saw

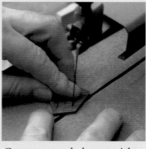

Finished petal construct

Tack glue inlay piece to base for scribing

Leaves & petals are book matched

To hang plaque on wall make hanger detail p27.

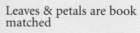
Tulip poplar (stems)
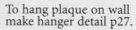
Tulip poplar (book matched)
Tulip poplar (book matched)

different color of leaves indicate grain simulation

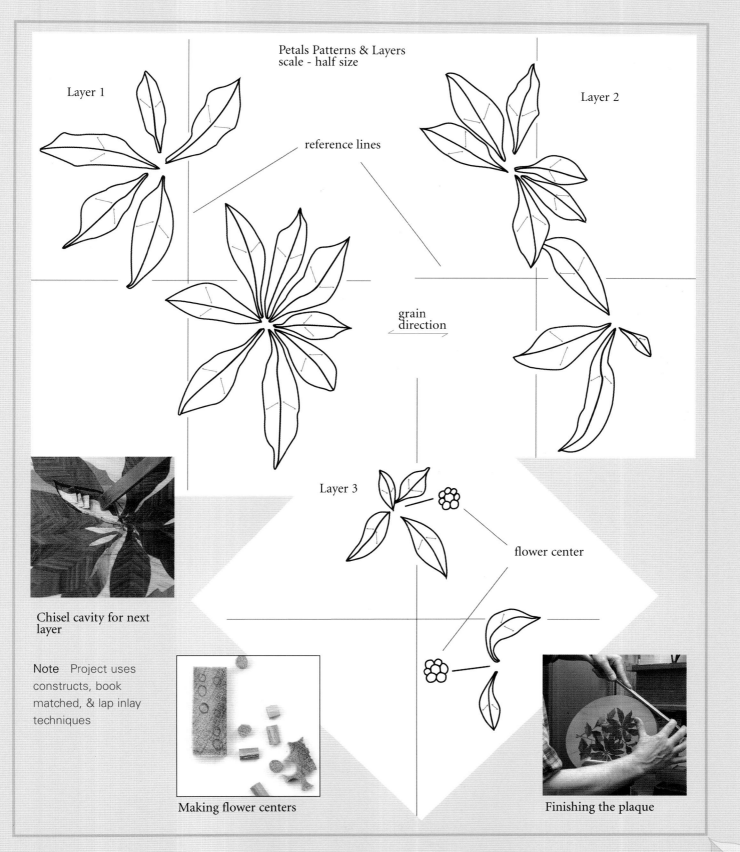

Petals Patterns & Layers
scale - half size

Layer 1

Layer 2

reference lines

grain
direction

Layer 3

flower center

Chisel cavity for next layer

Note   Project uses constructs, book matched, & lap inlay techniques

Making flower centers

Finishing the plaque

Petals choices, location, & steps
not to scale

step 1

step 2

step 3

step 4

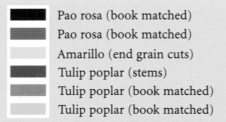
Pao rosa (book matched)
Pao rosa (book matched)
Amarillo (end grain cuts)
Tulip poplar (stems)
Tulip poplar (book matched)
Tulip poplar (book matched)

Lazy Susan

This tray is versatile for entertaining or family serving and fairly easy to make. The maple leaves are inlaid as constructs. Their size and complex shape are fairly difficult to inlay.

Base Material
Elm 2 ft x 1 ft x 1¼ in
Inlay Materials
American walnut, bloodwood, tulip poplar, osage orange, amarillo

Tray Construction

1 Using a ¼ in router fitted with a radius arm and ¼ in straight-cut bit scribe 2 disks from 1¼ in (dressed to 1 in thickness) tray material.

> Note   You can cut the disks free from the rough stock by making a series of cuts, each slightly deeper than the other. (¼ in at each pass). I cut to a depth of ½ in and completed cutting disks with a portable jigsaw (diagram 1 & 2). The edge of the disks can be brought to the desired diameter and sanded smooth on a disk sander (diagram 3).

2 Cutting the disks free can be postponed until after diagram 5. It is easier to clamp and hold a rectangular piece in place than a round piece.

3 Using ¼ in router arm and moving pivot point in ⅜ in, make radius cut using ¾ in straight-cut bit (diagram 4). This cut provides enough clearance from outside edge to allow remaining portion of tray to be routed out freehand.

4 When removing remainder of material from tray, leave several narrow ridges to support the router base (diagram 5). Leave the counter pivot sight intact so that if the depth has to be adjusted at any time, re-shaping is possible. Tear-outs or nicks can be avoided by making many shallow cuts to achieve desired depth.

5 When routing is complete, remove ridges with hand tools (shallow curved gouge chisel to trim ridge flush, then sand).

6 Using ¼ in round over router bit with guide bearing, round over top inside and outside edges of tray rim (do this freehand or place router into router table, see diagram 6).

Diagram 1

Note - diagrams 1 - 10 not to scale

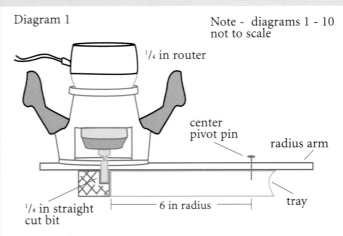

¼ in router

center pivot pin

radius arm

¼ in straight cut bit

6 in radius

tray

Diagram 2

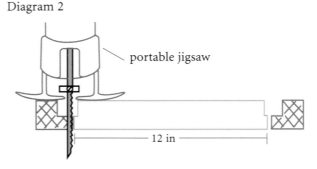

portable jigsaw

12 in

Diagram 3

disk sander

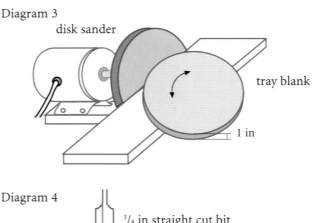

tray blank

1 in

Diagram 4

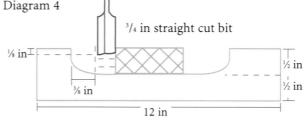

¾ in straight cut bit

⅛ in

½ in

½ in

⅜ in

12 in

Base Construction

1. Cut disk for base of lazy susan (diagram 1 & 2). Set radius arm of router at 3⅛ in (diagram 7). Finish outside edge with disk sander (diagram 3).
2. See profile of base plate (diagram 8). Set router table (diagram 9). Place ¾ in core box bit in router and set to required depth. Adjust V-shape router fence to provide support against which base can be rotated. Orient it square to router bit.

> Note To produce an accurate inside-edge cut, position the V-fence so that the center of your work is between the router bit and the V-fence (as shown in diagram 9). To produce an accurate outside-edge cut, position the V-fence so that the router bit is now between the V-fence and the center of your work.

3. Adjust distance of fence so that when disk is slowly placed on top of router bit and rotated, it will cut a groove ¾ in from outside edge of disk.
4. Using straightcut router bit, cut the top profile of the base in same way as bottom profile.
5. See diagram 10 to show mounting of lazy susan on bearing.

Inlay Procedure

1. See pattern (p54) for maple leaves. Follow inlay procedure (p14).
2. Leaves can be constructed from book matched material or assembled from angle cut material of different shades.
3. Form center vein profile on one side (photo 1). Match this profile to a wide piece of wood and glue together (photo 2). Direction of grain should not match either side of leaf. Use a piece of wood slightly different in color.
4. After glued pieces have set, cut away excess to form vein and stem of leaf (diagram 11 & 12).
5. Add 3rd piece matching the new profile of the vein. Glue together. When set cut out profile of leaf from construct pieces (photo 4). Make the 4 leaves in the same manner.
6. Osage orange leaf shown has amarillo stem. Note All leaves differ from each other for this tray - they are not exact copies of each other.
7. Glue leaf to tray (photo 5). Scribe around it. Lift off. Proceed to inlay (p14).

> Note Each leaf part is cut from different woods. Leaves are cut on a bias angle of 50°. Inlays of this size are the maximum handled by the inlay press in this book. Larger size inlays require a larger press.

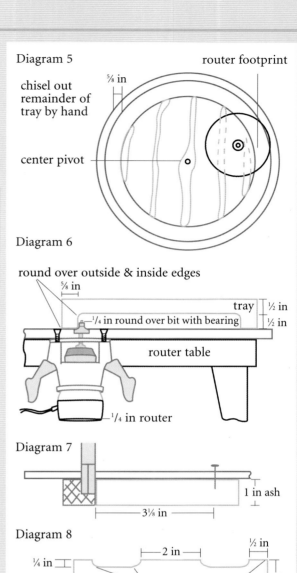

Diagram 5

router footprint
⅝ in
chisel out remainder of tray by hand
center pivot

Diagram 6

round over outside & inside edges
⅝ in
¼ in round over bit with bearing
tray ½ in ½ in
router table
¼ in router

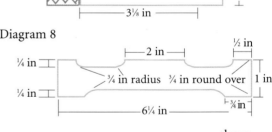

Diagram 7

1 in ash
3⅛ in

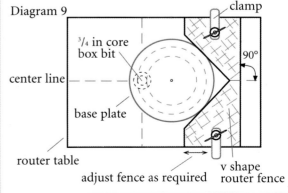

Diagram 8

2 in ½ in
¼ in
¾ in radius ¾ in round over 1 in
¼ in
6¼ in ¾ in

Diagram 9

clamp
¾ in core box bit
90°
center line
base plate
router table
adjust fence as required
v shape router fence

Diagram 10
not to scale

the ⅝ in access hole is drilled through the base to allow attachment of the tray to the top half of the bearing

⅝ in access hole

trim corner to fit base

Lazy susan

bearing

4 in

base of tray

attach bearing with ⅝ in x #6 sheet metal screws

Leaf Pattern to scale

grain direction

Diagram 11

Diagram 12

Diagram 11 & 12 not to scale

glue together

cut away

1 Make center rib of leaf construct

2 Glue leaf pieces together and clamp

3 Use spindle sander to adjust thickness of stem

4 Cut out leaf from construct using scroll saw

Note Project uses construct technique

5 Tack glue leaf on tray and scribe around it

Trinket Boxes

These boxes are relatively easy to make. The contrast of wood grains on the inlay pieces provides interest. Boxes can be any size according to material on hand.

Base Material

1 Maple box

    4 in x 2⅞ in x 1⅞ in x ⁵⁄₁₆ in thick

    top & bottom - 4½ in x 3⅜ in x ½ in

2 Cherry wood box

    3⅝ in x 2¾ in x 1⅞ in x ¼ in thick

    top and bottom - 3¼ in x 4⅛ in x ½ in

Inlay Material

Bloodwood, poplar, amarillo, red oak, mahogany, black walnut, satin walnut,

Base Construction

> Note When making oak leaf, choose oak piece different from box top and bottom or contrast grain and color. Cut the two acorn caps from different pieces of mahogany.

1 Adjust fence on router table to cut wood pieces to desired length (see pattern diagram) using ¼ in straight cut bit and backing block.

2 Set up router table as shown in diagram 3. Cut 45° angle on ends of each piece used for sides of box. Use a backing block to support each piece as it passes through router.

3 Cut width of each piece same way you cut length. Trim any torn edges.

4 Cut ⅛ in x ⅛ in rabbet on bottom edge of each side and end piece (diagram 1).

5 Sand ends true on disk sander (diagram 4) and adjust each piece to length required.

6 Assemble sides of box without glue. Cut a scrap piece of wood the exact internal dimensions of the box and make sure all corners are 90° so box is square when you glue it.

7 Glue box together with white carpenter's glue. Clamp (diagram 5). Use a strong elastic restraint on clamping blocks to secure corners. Allow to dry.

8 Sand outside of box on disk sander to true box sides to an even thickness.

9 Fit bottom of box, as shown (diagram 2).

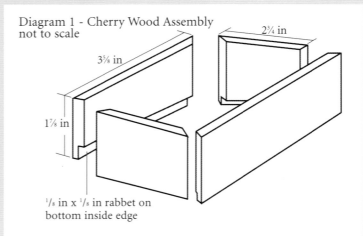

Diagram 1 - Cherry Wood Assembly
not to scale

2¾ in

3⅝ in

1⅞ in

⅛ in x ⅛ in rabbet on bottom inside edge

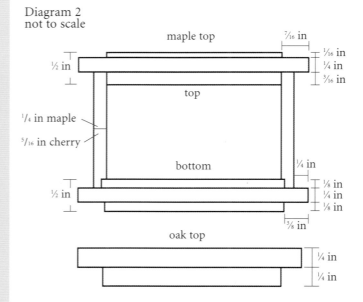

Diagram 2
not to scale

maple top

⁷⁄₁₆ in

½ in

¹⁄₁₆ in

¼ in

³⁄₁₆ in

top

¼ in maple

⁵⁄₁₆ in cherry

bottom

¼ in

½ in

⅛ in

¼ in

⅛ in

⅜ in

oak top

¼ in

¼ in

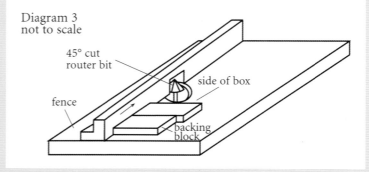

Diagram 3
not to scale

45° cut router bit

side of box

fence

backing block

Inlay Procedure

> Note   Inlay top of box before it is shaped to finished style so any molded features will not be compromised by sanding of inlay.

Flower inlay

1 Each leaf is made of 2 pieces of wood which are assembled as a construct (p16) before leaf is inlaid. (diagram 6). Cut the wood pieces down the center (detail c) to leave one half grain pattern the mirror of the other which is called book matching.

2 Leaf halves are fitted together with matching curve cuts (I scroll saw and spindle sand (detail e). Cut positive or negative side, then hand fit opposite side. Hold halves fitted together up to light to check fit. Adjust with small file until no light shines through. Glue with white carpenter's glue. Clamp. Allow to set 5 to 10 minutes. Transfer (p12) leaf pattern to wood and cut out.

3 Lay sanding pad on workbench and sand wood inlay construct pieces to ³⁄₁₆ in thickness. Inlay leaves to bottom of cavities.

4 Transfer (p12) flower petals pattern to selected wood. Cut out. Sand petals to ³⁄₁₆ in thickness. Follow inlay procedures (p14). Petals are inlaid over leaves.

5 Cut and shape small end grain piece from amarillo for center of flower. Inlay in place.

6 Using ½ in straight cutting router bit, mill outside edge of box top to leave the center inlay slightly raised. Rout the bottom edge to allow it to fit into box (diagram 2, p56).

Oak Leaf Inlay

1 Rough cut out inlay wood. Prepare 3 separate constructs (oak leaf diagram, step 1). Sand each construct to ³⁄₁₆ in thickness.

2 Follow inlay procedure on p14.

3 Inlay branch construct, then oak leaf construct, then acorn constructs.

4 Optional To achieve appearance that leaf is attached to back of branch, inlay leaf and the branch over top.

5 Using ½ in straight cut router bit in the router table, router the bottom edge of the inlaid lid to fit box.

> Note   Use a sharp chisel to scrape away machine marks.

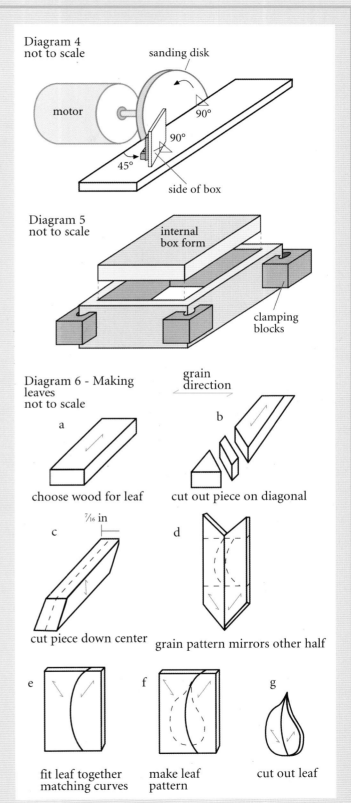

Diagram 4
not to scale

sanding disk

motor

90°

90°

45°

side of box

Diagram 5
not to scale

internal
box form

clamping
blocks

Diagram 6 - Making leaves
not to scale

grain direction

a

choose wood for leaf

b

cut out piece on diagonal

c

⁷⁄₁₆ in

cut piece down center

d

grain pattern mirrors other half

e

fit leaf together
matching curves

f

make leaf
pattern

g

cut out leaf

Flower Box Pattern
scale - actual size

grain
direction

Flower Box - wood choices & steps
not to scale

step 1

step 2

step 3

leaves book
matched see p16

	Maple
	Bloodwood
	Tulip poplar(book matched)
	Tulip poplar (book matched)
	Amarillo

Oak Leaf Box Pattern
scale - actual size

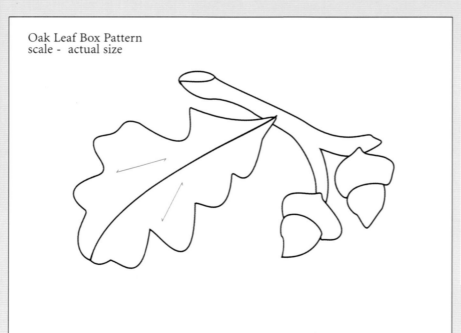

Oak Leaf Box - wood choices & steps
not to scale

step 1

branch
constructs

acorn constructs

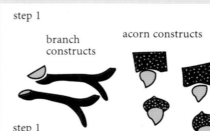

step 1

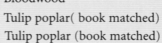

oak leaf construct - see p16

step 2

Note   Project uses book match,
constructs, & lap inlay techniques

	Cherry
	Mahogany (end grain cuts)
	Satin walnut
	Red oak
	Black walnut

Recipe Box

For the recipe box I chose a B grade oak to give the project an antique character. The trailing inlays look well on the oak.

Base Material
Red oak (B grade) 6 in x 40 in x ⅜ in
Inlay Material
Greenheart, tulip poplar, amarillo, black walnut, birch

> Note   Inlay of box top can be done before box is assembled.

Box Construction

1 Using red oak, assemble the box as shown in diagram 1.
2 Make ½ in rabbet cut in 4 sides of box before assembly. Cuts should not follow through to outside edges on front or back panels.
3 Follow the same procedure to cut rabbet to accept bottom of box. Do not carry the cut through the edges of the front or back panels.
4 When box is assembled, cut top off using ⅛ in router bit. This will leave ³⁄₁₆ in inside rabbet on top and bottom sections of box (see detail B).
5 Trim inside edge of bottom section of box with ⅜ in x ³⁄₁₆ in walnut strip.
6 Glue this strip into ³⁄₁₆ in x ³⁄₁₆ in rabbet (see detail C). For end detail of these strips see diagram 2, detail D.
7 See diagram 3 for box handle construction. Handles are fitted with splines and glued to sides of box.
8 I chose solid brass hasp with hook ¾ in x 2¾ in and 2 butterfly hinges 1⁵⁄₁₆ in x 2¼ in. However, alternative hardware can be used.

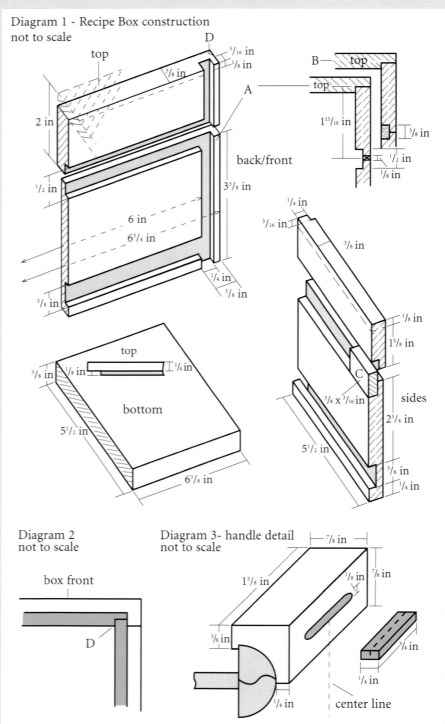

Diagram 1 - Recipe Box construction
not to scale

Diagram 2
not to scale

Diagram 3- handle detail
not to scale

Inlay Procedure

1 Inlay top before box is assembled. Inlay front and side panels after box is assembled and top is separated.

2 Transfer (p12) pattern for inlay pieces to chosen woods. Cut out. Proceed with inlay steps outlined on p14.

3 Construct leaves for inlay same as shown on p16.

4 Construct end of branch detail (diagram 4, p65) and flowers (diagram 5). For flowers, carve one shape from a thick block of birch and then cut a number of identical pieces and shape each flower separately. This works well for small flower petals.

5 Use amarillo for flower centers. Its end cut grain has very little growth ring detail and it has the appearance of fine yellow fuzz.

6 Pressing inlays into sides of box is different than for top. I used a C-clamp padded with soft wood blocks.

7 Make inlay pear of greenheart wood which is hard and brittle. The leaves that overlay the greenheart are more difficult to inlay. Scribe around the leaf shape, cut the shoulder, then cut out the cavity in the center of the scribed line (make a release cut, p 17), then trim the wood back to the shoulder.

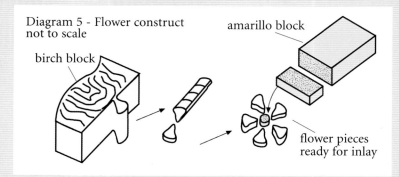

Diagram 5 - Flower construct not to scale

birch block   amarillo block

flower pieces ready for inlay

1 Scribe around leaf pattern piece with sharp knife

2 Remove pattern piece and recut scribed line, cut shoulder

3 Cut out cavity

4 File second bevel on inlay piece

C-clamp padded with soft wood blocks

5 Glue sides and bottom of cavity and inlay piece

6 Sand inlay piece smooth, remove glue, sand flush

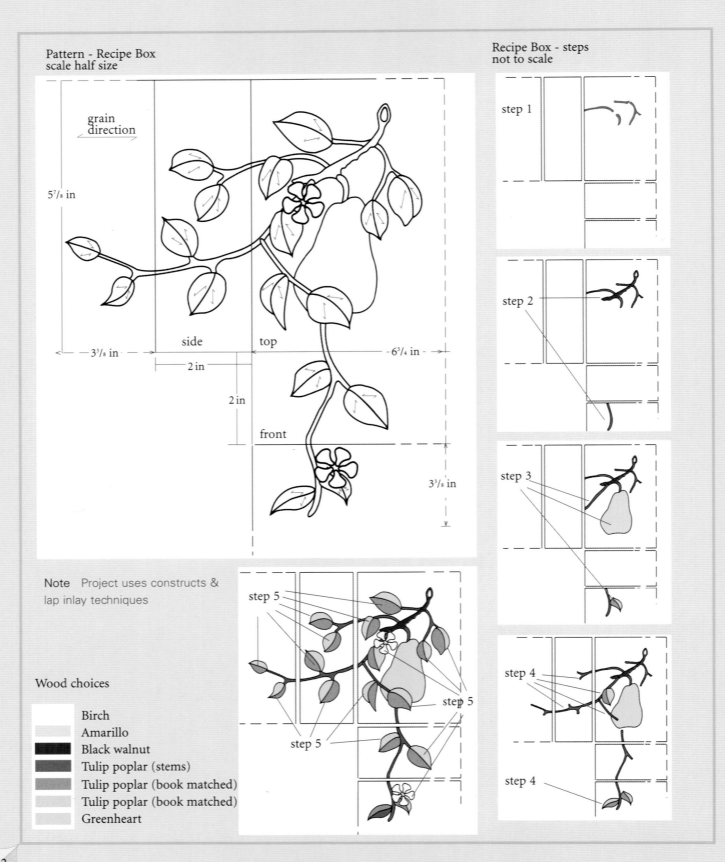

Pattern - Recipe Box
scale half size

grain
direction

$5^7/_8$ in

$3^3/_8$ in

side

top

2 in

2 in

front

$6^3/_4$ in

$3^3/_8$ in

Recipe Box - steps
not to scale

step 1

step 2

step 3

step 4

step 4

Note   Project uses constructs &
lap inlay techniques

step 5

step 5

step 5

step 5

Wood choices

Birch
Amarillo
Black walnut
Tulip poplar (stems)
Tulip poplar (book matched)
Tulip poplar (book matched)
Greenheart

Recipe Book Stand

T he materials for this project are the same as for the Recipe Box project. This stand is cut from one piece of wood and has a unique design that folds flat for storage.

Base Material
Red oak 9 in x 14 in x ¹³⁄₁₆ in
Inlay Material
Greenheart, tulip poplar, amarillo, black walnut, birch

Stand Construction

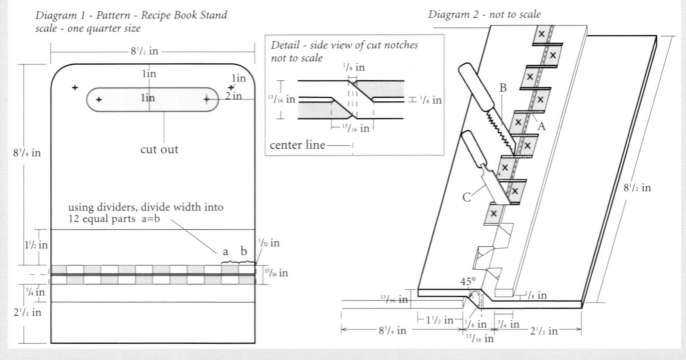

Diagram 1 - Pattern - Recipe Book Stand
scale - one quarter size

8¹⁄₂ in

1in

1in

1in
2 in

cut out

8³⁄₄ in

using dividers, divide width into
12 equal parts a=b

1¹⁄₂ in

a   b   ¹⁄₃₂ in

¹³⁄₁₆ in

³⁄₄ in

2¹⁄₂ in

Detail - side view of cut notches
not to scale

¹⁄₈ in

¹³⁄₁₆ in   ¹⁄₈ in

¹³⁄₁₆ in

center line

Diagram 2 - not to scale

B

A

8¹⁄₂ in

C

45°

¹³⁄₁₆ in   ¹⁄₈ in

8³⁄₄ in   1¹⁄₂ in   ¹⁄₈ in   ³⁄₄ in   2¹⁄₂ in
            ¹³⁄₁₆ in

1 See dimensional drawing of book stand (diagram 1). The length of the hinged notch section depends on the thickness of the material (here ¹³⁄₁₆ in) used to make the stand.

2 Follow the steps shown in diagram 2 to cut the hinge section.

> Note   The length of the notched section will always be equal to the thickness of the material used to achieve a 90° hinge opening. The number of notches over the width of the stand is determined by the width of the chisel (here ¾ in) used to cut the notches.

3 Drill a series of holes side by side along each slot mark using ¹⁄₁₆ in drill bit. Drill to a depth slightly more than ½ the thickness of the wood. Full depth penetration is achieved by drilling the remainder of the thickness from the opposite side. See A.

Hacksaw blades & handle

I use a drill press with a fence to position the stand. Use the fence to drill each slot on each side and from each edge before setting the fence position to drill the next slot pair. Start from the outside edges and work towards the center of the stand.

The Art of Wood Inlay

Note Drilling the full thickness from one side is difficult because a ¹⁄₁₆ in drill bit will wander off the mark and not always exit on the mark on the other side.

4 Use ½ length of a 12 in hacksaw blade ground to a point and fashioned with a handle to complete cutting of the slots. See B, diagram 2.
5 Complete the operation using ¹⁄₁₆ in thick file to clean up each slot to a smooth finish. See C, diagram 2.
6 Construct this simple jig (diagram 3) to assist carving out each notch, keeping the angle cuts in line and at the proper pitch.

Note The top portion of the jig (the pitch block) is fastened to a bottom board with adjustable bolts. Placing the book stand in the jig and tightening the bolts will make the cutting of the notches much easier than trying to cut each one separately.

7 Diagram 3 shows the edge of the pitch block used to align and cut the vertical edges and the edge of the pitch block used to cut the angles. See D.
8 After the notches have been cut, the hinge is completed by ripping the material down the center from either end until the notches are reached. See E.

Inlay Procedure

1 Transfer (p12) pattern of inlay pieces to chosen woods and cut out. Proceed with inlay steps p14.
2 See diagram 4 for method used to construct branch detail. This step is well worth the extra effort.
3 Construct flower as shown in Recipe Box project, p61. See diagrams p66 for inlay materials and steps required.

Note Project uses constructs, book match, & lap inlay techniques

Cutting slots   *Cutting slots*

Chisel out notches   *Chiseled notches*

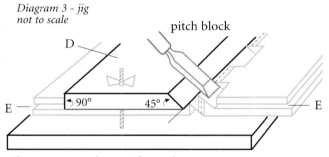
Diagram 3 - jig not to scale

pitch block

D

E — 90° 45° — E

Shows proper marking out for notches

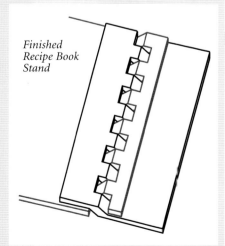
Finished Recipe Book Stand

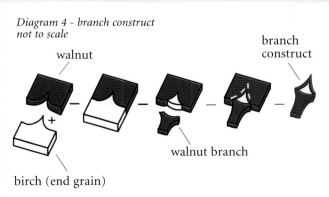
Diagram 4 - branch construct not to scale

walnut

branch construct

walnut branch

birch (end grain)

grain
direction

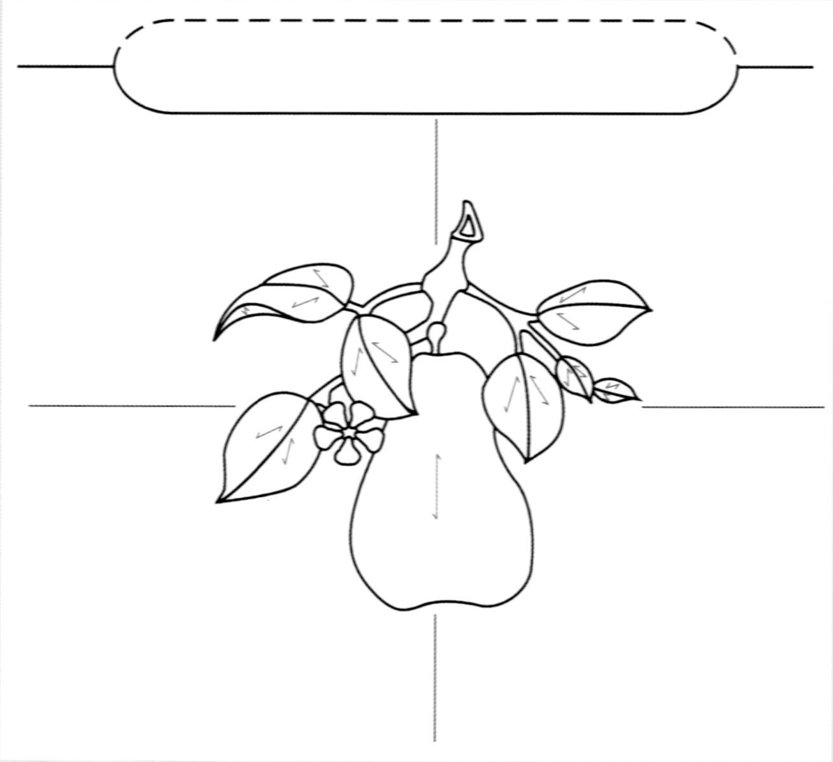

step 1

step 2

step 3

step 4

step 6

step 5

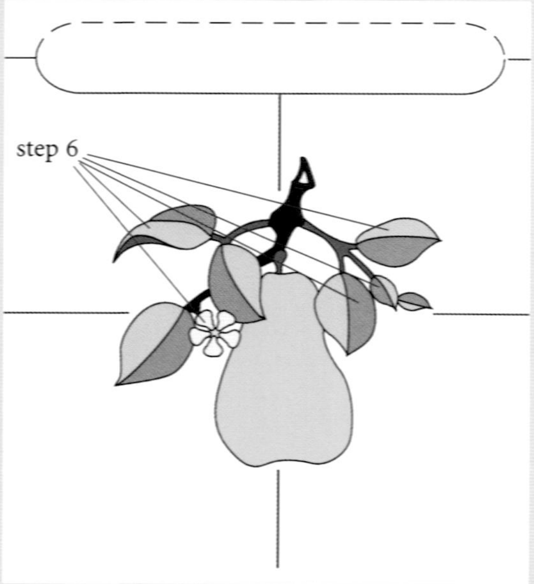

Wood choices

	Birch
	Amarillo
	Black walnut
	Tulip poplar
	Tulip poplar (book matched)
	Tulip poplar (book matched)
	Greenheart

Watering Can Tray

This round tray has a fitted block trim that makes a decorative edge. The jig helps to cut the blocks accurately. Base wood is cut for the most interesting grain pattern.

Base Material
Elm

Inlay Material
Mahogany, locust, Brazilian rosewood, pernambuco, aromatic cedar, caragana, tulip poplar, moradillo

Tray Construction

Carve base of tray to a thickness of ¼ in. Inlays should not be deeper than 50% of base thickness. Base thickness determines what thickness inlays should be.

1 Using a straight cut router bit define the inside edge of the decorative trim blocks. For this cut use full width of the router bit to insure a clean sharp edge. Mount router on a radius arm and pivot from the center of the tray blank.

2 Using the same technique and a smaller diameter router bit, cut down into the tray blank to define the outside diameter of the tray.

3 Using hand jigsaw cut tray free from blank.

4 Using jig set-up shown, cut a number of edge blocks sufficient to circle tray. Using disk sander taper edges of each block so they fit together side by side around tray edge. When fit is accurate glue each block in place with a rub fit and hold each block in place for a minute (no clamping required).

5 Sand blocks flush to surface after glue has completely set. Sand edge flush using disk sander.

6 Continue to hollow out tray as described for Lazy Susan tray.

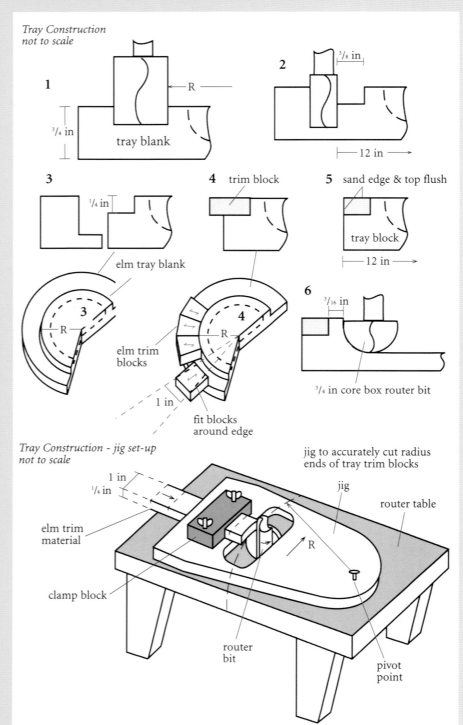

Tray Construction
not to scale

1   tray blank   R   ¾ in

2   ⅜ in   12 in

3   ¼ in

4   trim block

5   sand edge & top flush   tray block   12 in

6   3/16 in   ¾ in core box router bit

3   R   elm tray blank

4   R   elm trim blocks   1 in   fit blocks around edge

Tray Construction - jig set-up
not to scale

1 in   ¼ in   elm trim material   clamp block   router bit

jig to accurately cut radius ends of tray trim blocks   jig   router table   R   pivot point

Inlay Procedure

1 Proceed to inlay pieces in order as shown in diagrams p70. Follow general inlay steps given on p14.

Note   The end grain earth shapes (inlay pieces 1 & 2 in diagram 1) can be inlaid into the shallow cavity if care is taken to carve cavity flat on the bottom and use an even clamping pressure to press pieces in place. Use a press block sized to cover the piece to be inlaid. Inlay should be approximately 115% of depth of cavity.

Note
Project uses constructs, book match, scorching, & lap inlay techniques

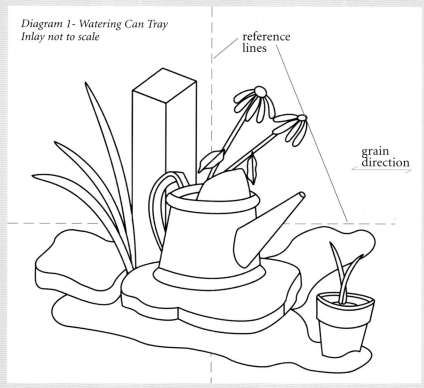

Diagram 1- Watering Can Tray
Inlay not to scale

reference lines

grain direction

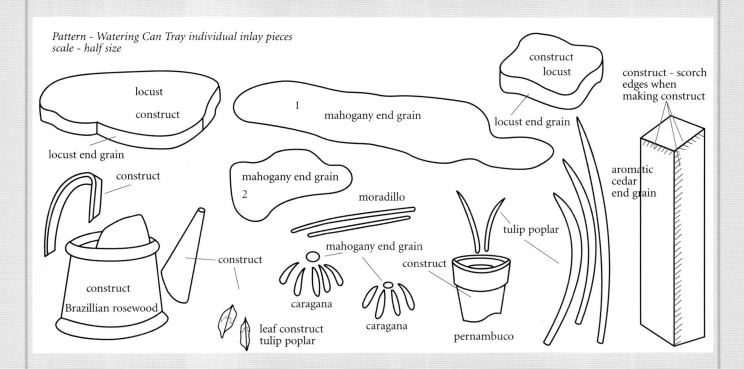

Pattern - Watering Can Tray individual inlay pieces
scale - half size

locust
construct

locust end grain

construct locust

locust end grain

construct - scorch edges when making construct

1 mahogany end grain

construct

mahogany end grain
2

moradillo

mahogany end grain

construct

tulip poplar

aromatic cedar end grain

construct

construct
Brazillian rosewood

leaf construct
tulip poplar

caragana

caragana

pernambuco

Watering Can Tray - steps not to scale

step 1

reference lines

step 2

step 3

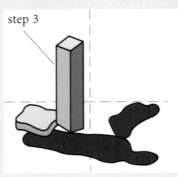

step 4

step 5

step 6

step 7

step 8

step 9

step 10

step 11

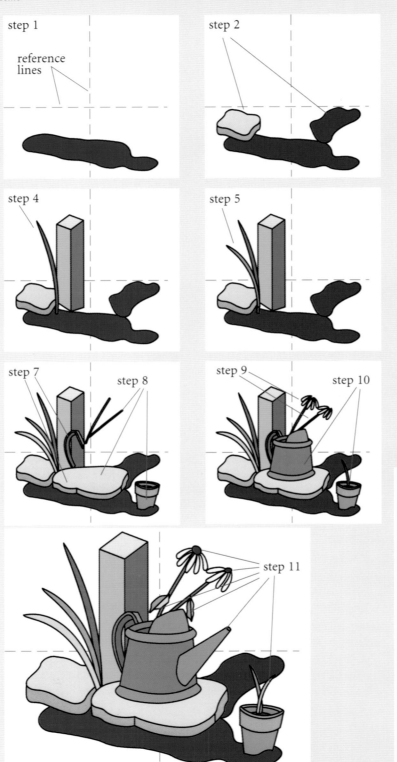

Wood choices

▉	Mahogany (end grain cut)
	Caragana
	Tulip poplar
	Tulip poplar (different shade)
	Tulip poplar (different shade)
	Brazilian rosewood
	Brazilian rosewood (different shade)
	Brazilian rosewood (different shade)
	Locust
	Locust (end grain)
	Pernambuco
	Pernambuco (different shade)
	Pernambuco (different shade)
	Aromatic cedar (end grain cut)
	Aromatic cedar
	Aromatic cedar (different shade)
	Moradillo

The Art of Wood Inlay

Fruit Tray

The yellow willow for the tray was given to me as a log from a neighbor. It is not a wood you can normally purchase from your local lumber yard but it interested me and I decided to experiment. I dried it for several months then cut and planed it into planks of various thicknesses and widths. If this wood is not available choose another suitable wood (cedar or pine). Note   Project uses constructs, lapping, book matched, & scorching techniques

Base Material

Yellow willow (glue two ³/₄ in thick planks together to make the 12 in tray)

Inlay Material

Russian olive, Manitoba maple, purpleheart, tulip poplar, hackberry

Tray Construction

1 Tray is 12 in diameter. See diagram 2. Cut profile of tray according to dimensions given.

2 Follow the same method of construction as given for Lazy Susan project, p52, diagrams 1 to 5.

Inlay Procedure

1 Inlay wooden slats first (Pattern A). Construct them as indicated (diagram 1). Cut strips of wood choosing interesting grain pattern and color. You can cut the edge piece and end grain piece from the same material used for the slat. If the grain matches too closely, use other cuts from the same wood source to make the appearance more interesting. Make the slat constructs as shown.

2 Transfer individual fruit patterns to appropriate inlay woods. Cut out. Follow inlay procedure on p14. Inlay the pieces in order given on p74.

3 If the glue joints appear seamless you can define the slats by scorching the edges of each slat with a wood burning tool before you assemble them. I also used this technique for the edges of the apple stem and plum to highlight them and make them easier to see. Experiment with this technique before you begin the inlay.

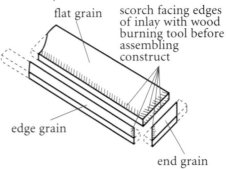

Diagram 1- Fruit Tray - slats not to scale

hackberry construct

flat grain

scorch facing edges of inlay with wood burning tool before assembling construct

edge grain

end grain

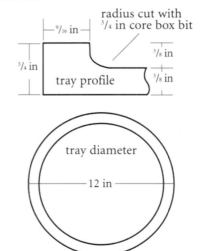

Diagram 2- Fruit Tray not to scale

radius cut with ³/₄ in core box bit

⁹/₁₆ in

³/₄ in

³/₈ in

³/₈ in

tray profile

tray diameter

12 in

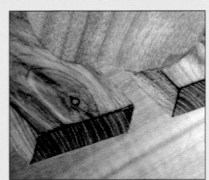

Shows scorching on inlaid planks

Note   Always test the scorching process on a piece of the wood to be used to get the effect you want. The inlay also has to fit. Inlay pieces shaped with sharp points (leaf) sometimes crush into place. If the piece is to be scorched on the edges be sure the cavity matches the inlay shape. The amount of scorching depends on the wattage of the wood burning tool and the temperature it can reach.

4 You will see that woods with a wide range of hardness can be inlaid successfully in the same project. Inlaying hardwoods (purpleheart) into a soft wood base (yellow willow, cedar, pine) can be inlaid almost flush with the base surface to minimize the amount of sanding needed. Fruits in this project are inlaid into the slats, not directly into willow base. Inlaying the hackberry slats into the yellow willow takes extra care. The end grain cuts of wood used on the ends of the slats are also very hard.

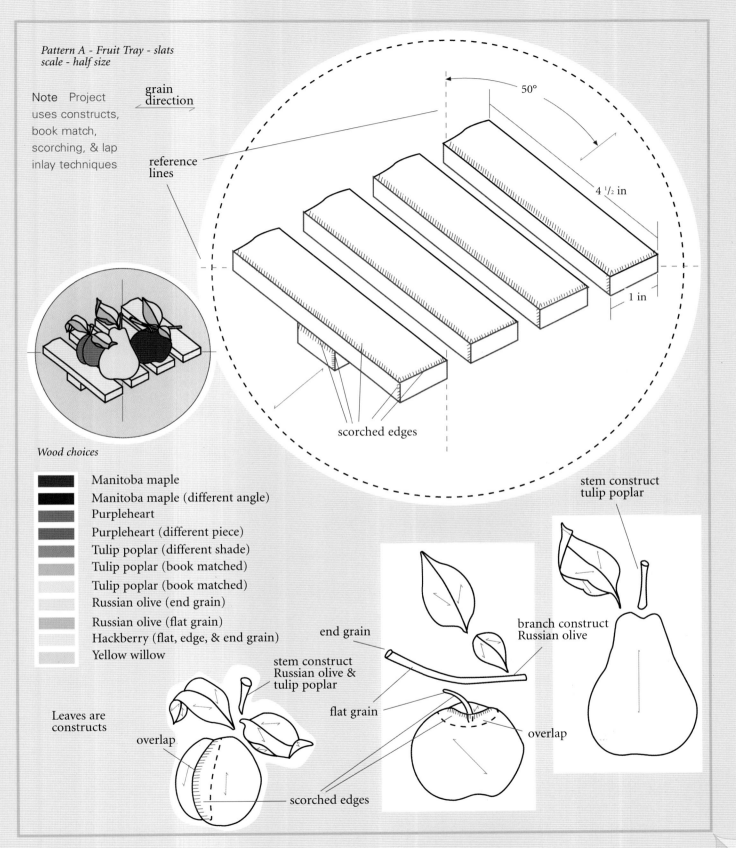

*Pattern A - Fruit Tray - slats
scale - half size*

Note Project uses constructs, book match, scorching, & lap inlay techniques

grain direction

reference lines

50°

4 1/2 in

1 in

scorched edges

Wood choices

- Manitoba maple
- Manitoba maple (different angle)
- Purpleheart
- Purpleheart (different piece)
- Tulip poplar (different shade)
- Tulip poplar (book matched)
- Tulip poplar (book matched)
- Russian olive (end grain)
- Russian olive (flat grain)
- Hackberry (flat, edge, & end grain)
- Yellow willow

Leaves are constructs

overlap

stem construct
Russian olive &
tulip poplar

scorched edges

end grain

flat grain

overlap

stem construct
tulip poplar

branch construct
Russian olive

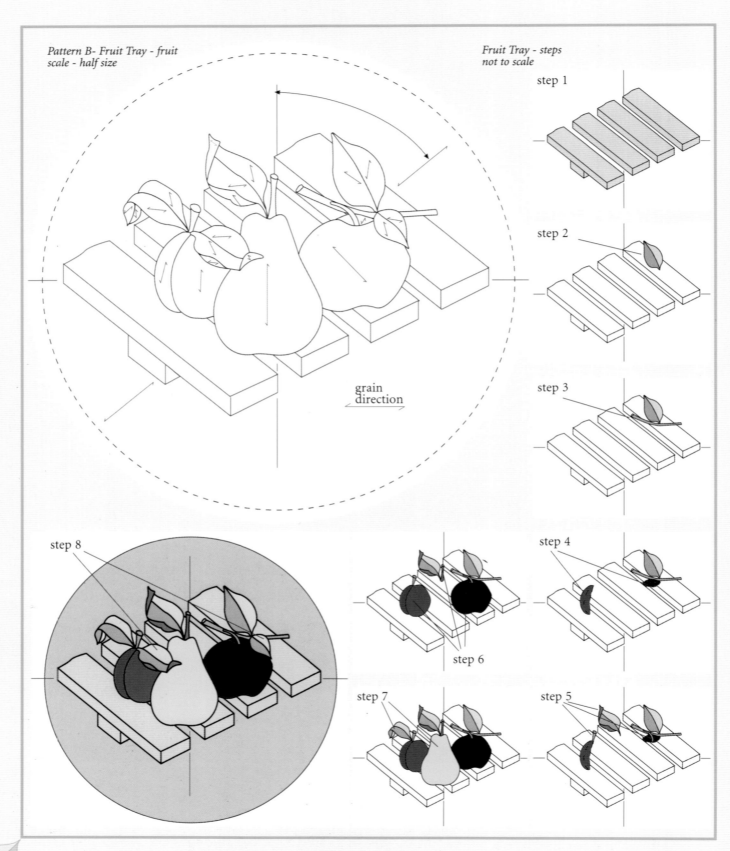

Pattern B- Fruit Tray - fruit
scale - half size

grain
direction

Fruit Tray - steps
not to scale

step 1

step 2

step 3

step 8

step 4

step 6

step 7

step 5

The Art of Wood Inlay

Card Box

Sometimes inlays made from the same material as the base wood look very elegant. To distinguish them place them at an interesting angle so the wood grain is different to catch the light in a special way.

Base Material
Hard maple   6 in x 3³/₄ in x 1¹/₄ in
Inlay Material
Black walnut, birch, pao rosa, Ceylon ebony

Box Construction
1 Box is carved from single piece of hard maple.
2 Cut a dovetail slot around 3 sides of the top edge of the box to accept the lid.
3 Cut piece of black walnut 6 in x 3³/₄ in x ¹/₂ in shaped with dovetail slots on 3 sides of the lid to form a sliding lid. See diagram 1 for construction details.

Inlay Procedure
1 See inlay pieces in diagram 2. Cut inlays for the sides of the box from the same maple wood that was used for the box (see diagram 1).
2 Sapwood layers from a birch tree are usually lighter in color with a fine straight grain. I chose it for the card sections because it matched the hardness of the walnut and the fine grain is appropriate.
3 Inlay the number 4 in two pieces .
4 Shape the spade from ebony and inlay two pieces, inlaying the stem first. Inlay all pieces according to directions on p14.

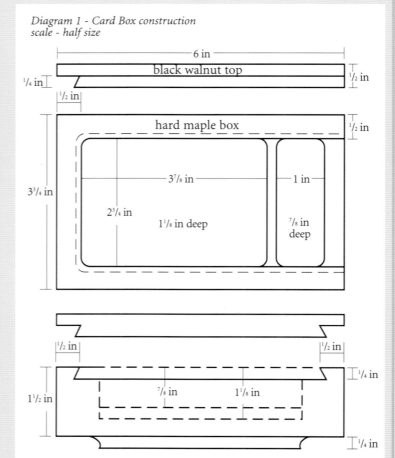

*Diagram 1 - Card Box construction
scale - half size*

6 in

black walnut top   ¹/₂ in

¹/₄ in   ¹/₂ in

hard maple box   ¹/₂ in

3³/₄ in   3⁷/₈ in   1 in

2³/₄ in   1¹/₈ in deep   ⁷/₈ in deep

¹/₂ in   ¹/₂ in

1¹/₂ in   ⁷/₈ in   1¹/₈ in   ¹/₄ in

¹/₄ in

1 Tack glue cut-out inlay on base & scribe around it with a sharp knife

2 Use chisel to cut out wood to receive inlay piece

3 Glue inlay in cavity and use wood block to press in place

Diagram 2 - Card Box Pattern - top & side
scale - half size

inlay walnut in walnut

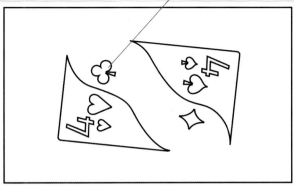

inlay maple in maple

Inlay card segments into box top. Inlay card numbers & symbols into assigned places using inlay procedures p14.

Maple inlay pieces are inlaid in maple base as aligned on grid

Card Box steps

step 1

step 2 step 3

Note   Project uses lap inlay technique

step 5

step 4

step 6

Wood choices

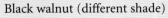

Ebony
Black walnut
Black walnut (different shade)
Maple
Maple (different shade)
Birch
Pao rosa

Card Box

Teddy Bear Step Stool

This stool is lightweight but sturdy and easy to move around to reach high cupboards or back shelves. The base of the stool is painted so lesser grade lumber may be used.

Base Material

Clear pine 12 ft x 8 in x1 in

Inlay Material

Pine, purpleheart, hackberry, chakte kok, pao rosa, Philippine mahogany, Honduras mahogany, amarillo, holly, tulip poplar, black walnut, satin walnut

Step Stool Construction

1 See diagram 1 for pattern details. Cut out all pieces from clear pine according to dimensions given. See detail A, B, and C.

2 Use white carpenter's glue on all joints. Use 1 in finishing nails to further stabilize the assembly. Set them just below the surface of the wood with a nail set and patch with wood filler. Sand smooth before painting.

3 To fasten the inlaid steps to the stool, use glue and screw the ¾ in x 1½ in blocks to the sides of the stool base.

4 Screw on each step from underneath with six 1 in number 8 wood screws and countersink the heads ¼ in (see diagram 1, detail D).

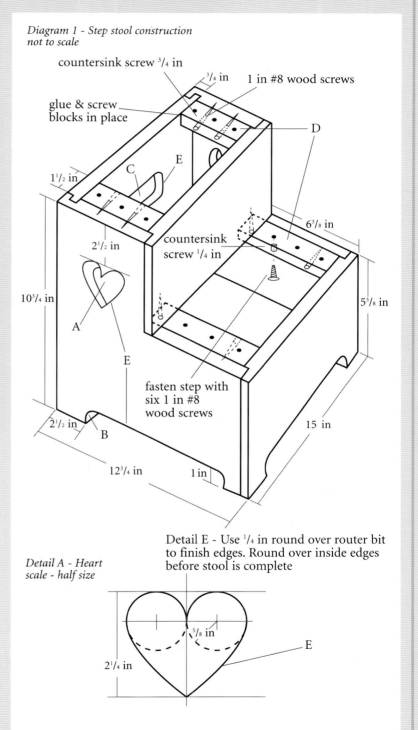

Diagram 1 - Step stool construction not to scale

countersink screw ³/₄ in

glue & screw blocks in place

countersink screw ¹/₄ in

fasten step with six 1 in #8 wood screws

³/₄ in   1 in #8 wood screws

D

E

C

E

1¹/₂ in

2¹/₂ in

6³/₈ in

10³/₄ in

A

E

5³/₈ in

2¹/₂ in   B

15 in

12³/₄ in   1 in

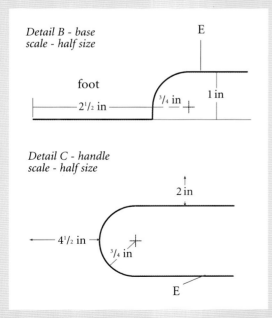

Detail B - base scale - half size

E

foot

2¹/₂ in   ³/₄ in   1 in

Detail C - handle scale - half size

2 in

4¹/₂ in   ³/₄ in

E

Detail A - Heart scale - half size

Detail E - Use ¹/₄ in round over router bit to finish edges. Round over inside edges before stool is complete

⁵/₈ in

E

2¹/₄ in

Diagram 2 -Pattern - Teddy Bear Step Stool - top step inlay
scale half size

16 in

use two reference lines to locate inlay on step

½ in

7 in

center line

use ¼ in round over router bit to finish edges

16 in

½ in

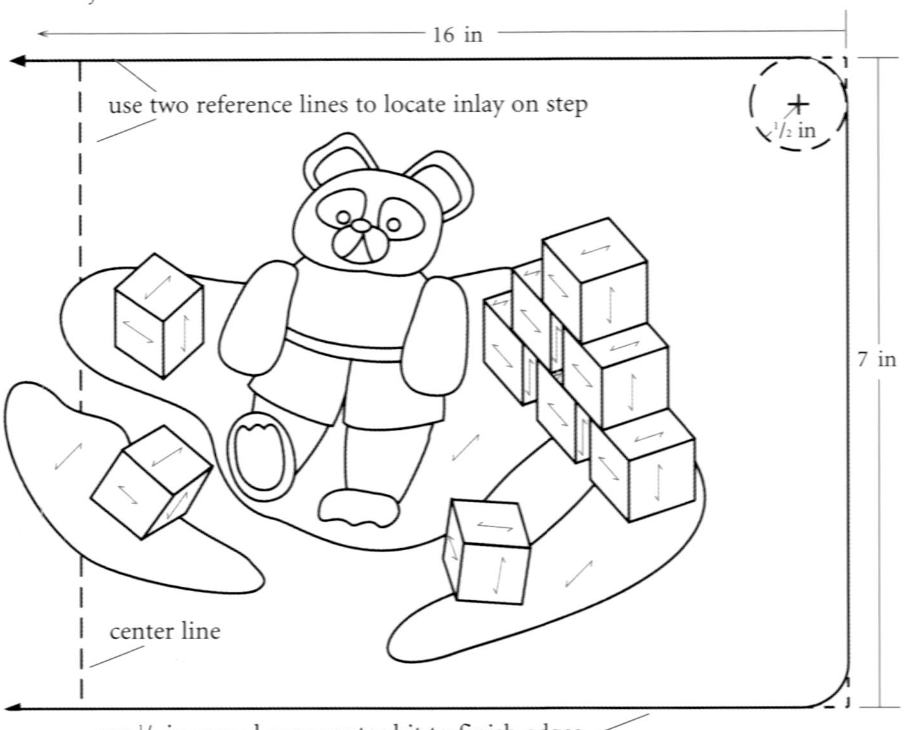

Diagram 3 - Pattern - Teddy Bear Step Stool - bottom step inlay
scale half size

center line

7 in

grain
direction

use ¼ in round over router bit to finish front & two side edges

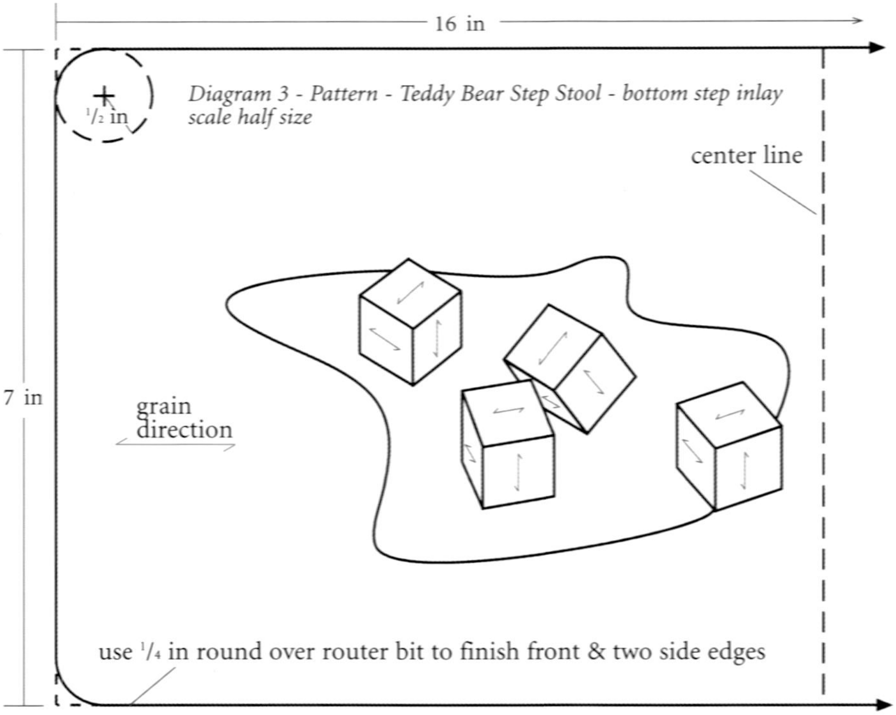

Inlay Procedure

1 Cut pieces of clear pine from the same plank used for the steps and dress to the inlay thickness of ³⁄₁₆ in. Shape pieces so their surface grain is biased to the grain of the steps, then inlay to give dimension to the picture.

2 Use (half size) patterns 2 and 3. Proceed with inlay techniques p14.

> Note Inlay pieces cut from end grain or biased grain mahogany are dressed to ¼ in. End grain pieces inlay much better in heavier thicknesses. Primary bevel of the inlay pieces should still be only one or two degrees, ¹⁄₁₆ in up from the bottom edge. Do a few test inlays into a scrap piece of pine. This will help decide how tight or loose the inlays should be. Adjust the tightness of inlays by increasing or decreasing the primary bevel.

3 See p82 for suggested order of inlay for the teddy bear.

4 See diagram 3 and 5 and construct the blocks individually. The angles of each block vary according to how they are drawn. The six colored blocks are identical in size with all angles equal. Overlay each block on top of the previous one until the stack is complete.

> Note Project uses constructs & lap inlay techniques

Inlay Order for Teddy Bear

1 Inlay outer ear pieces.
2 Inlay center ear pieces (end grain cut Honduras mahogany). Use same method to inlay two leg pieces.
3 Inlay upper body pieces.
4 Overlay head piece.
5 Overlay shorts (two pieces chakte kok).
6 Overlay belt covering joint between upper body and shorts (black walnut).
7 Inlay arms and feet overlaying upper body and leg pieces.
8 Inlay eye sockets (satin walnut).
9 Using end grain cuts (as in ear center pieces) inlay nose piece and sole piece.
10 Complete teddy bear by inlaying eye and nose detail (black walnut).

Bias cut Philippine mahogany

End grain cut Honduras mahogany

*Diagram 4 - Pattern - Teddy Bear Step Stool - teddy bear
scale full size*

grain
direction

bias cut mahogany for teddy bear parts

Inlay order - Teddy bear

step 1

step 2

step 3

step 4

step 5

step 6

step 8

step 7

step 9

step 10

Diagram 5 -Block construction-
not to scale

make each block individually

the angles of each single
block are different

grain
direction

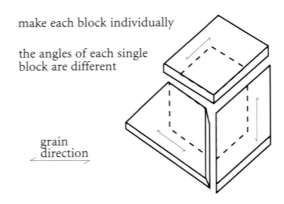

the stack of 6 colored blocks are all the same angles

assemble or construct the 6 blocks identically

the stack is formed by
overlaying one block
on top of the next

identical
shaped blocks

inlay each block
overlapping the next

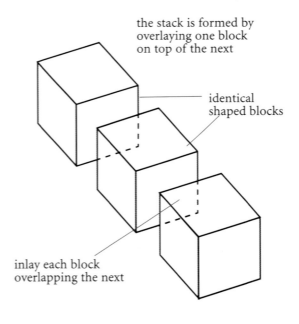

Wood choices - Teddy bear

	Satin walnut
	Black walnut
	Chakte kok
	Chakte kok (different angle)
	Honduras mahogany (end grain cut) inside ears, snout, & foot pad
	Philippine mahogany (bias cut)
	Philippine mahogany (bias cut)

The Art of Wood Inlay

Wood choices - Teddy Bear Step Stool - top

☐	Pine
▨	Tulip poplar
▨	Tulip poplar (different angle)
▨	Tulip poplar (different angle)
☐	Amarillo
☐	Amarillo (different angle)
☐	Amarillo (different angle)
■	Pao rosa
■	Pao rosa (different angle)
▨	Pao rosa (different angle)
▨	Purpleheart
▨	Purpleheart (different angle)
▨	Purpleheart (different angle)
☐	Hackberry
▨	Hackberry (different angle)
▨	Hackberry (different angle)
☐	Holly
☐	Holly (different angle)
☐	Holly (different angle)
▨	Pernambuco
▨	Pernambuco (different angle)
▨	Pernambuco (different angle)

Steps - Teddy Bear Step Stool - top

step 1

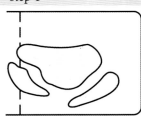

step 2

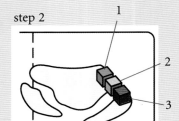

step 3

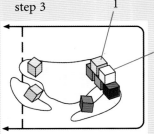

step 4

Steps - Teddy Bear Step Stool - top

step 1

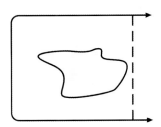

step 2

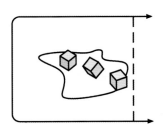

step 3

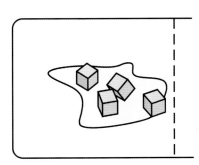

Wood choices - Teddy bear step stool - bottom step

☐	Pine
☐	Hackberry
▨	Hackberry (different angle)
▨	Hackberry (different angle)

Round Acorn Box

T his project is an example of deep inlay. The inlays are constructed from ¹/₂ in material and inlaid their entire thickness. The techniques involve doing an inlay into a surface that will be rounded. The process resembles chiseling out a mortise to make a mortise and tenon joint. But here the mortise is free-form shape rather than a rectangle. Deep inlays can be pressed into a blind cavity (that has a bottom). For this project I cut the cavity completely through the ¹/₂ in material. Inlays are done in ¹/₂ in thick panel strip that accommodated all six panels. See diagram 4.

Base Material
Red oak ¹/₂ in x 2 ¹/₂ in x 12 in
Maple 1³/₄ in x 4 in for armature of box
Black walnut ¹/₈ in thick for accent of panel partitions, box top, bottom facings

Inlay Material
Satin walnut, tulip poplar, mahogany

> **Note**   Red oak came from 2 sources - 1 piece for inlay panels, 1 for top and bottom. However, same piece can be used for both.

Note   Project uses constructs & deep inlay techniques

Box Construction
Make box according to dimensions given in diagram.

Box Armature Construction

1 Drill symmetrical holes in the armature in order to carve out as much wood as possible from the center of the box and still leave enough behind to handle the box through its construction. Drill the holes before cutting away the armature from the hard maple wood block (see diagram 1).

2 Cut and turn two more circular blocks from the same material or other wood stock of suitable dimension.

3 Turn the second block the thickness of a piece of 80 grit sandpaper smaller than the box armature and turn the third block 2¾ in diameter. Use it to finish sanding the interior of the finished box before the bottom is attached and after the webs of the armature are cut away. In these two blocks drill only the center ¼ in hole.

4 To turn armatures see diagram 2. Drilling a ¼ in hole into a hardwood base and then clamping it to the table of a disk sander is all the jig-making required to turn the armature blanks. Insert a ¼ in steel drill bit through the armature and into the jig. The pivot point is solid and by gradually moving the base block into the wheel a round block can be turned (see diagram 3). Drilling a few holes through the secondary sanding blocks makes them easier to handle while turning.

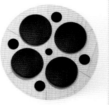

Drilled holes in block

Armature cut away from block

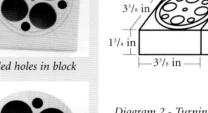

Diagram 1 - Armature construction not to scale

3³/₈ in
1³/₄ in
3³/₈ in

Diagram 2 - Turning armature not to scale

¼ in drill bit
pivot
armature   disk sander
jig   block   table

Diagram 3 - Armature block scale - half size

3³/₈ in
1¹/₈ in hole
³/₈ in hole
¼ in

Sanding the box armature on disk sander

Wrapping of second armature with 80 grit sandpaper

Sanding jig armature & mandrel

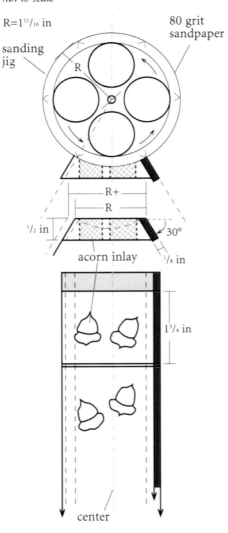

Diagram 4 - Calculating dimensions of inlay panels

not to scale

R=1¹¹/₁₆ in

sanding jig

R

80 grit sandpaper

R+

R

½ in

30°

acorn inlay

⅛ in

1³/₄ in

center

Diagram 5 - Calculations
not to scale

R+

R

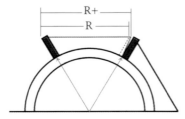

Inlaid single panel before shaping on sanding jig

5 Armature wall is ¼ in thick to start but can be trimmed down to any thickness you wish.

6 Now calculate the dimensions of the inlay panels. Turn the armature as shown (diagram 4). For a six-sided box divide the circumference of the armature by using the radius measurement as a reference. Each point of the circumference of the circle is equal to the radius measurement. Using ½ in thick material for the panel blocks and drawing a radius curve equal to that of the armature through the center of the block will leave approximately ¼ in finished inlaid panel. The width of the panel can be determined by using the R measurement for the inside length and projecting the corners outward 30°.

7 The R+ dimension adds a little extra to the width and allows you to fit them together accurately on the armature (see diagram 5). The final width will depend upon the thickness of the partition strip fitted between the panels. I used a ⅛ in thick strip of walnut to accent the oak panels (diagram 4). This strip is added after the edges of the panel are trimmed to 30°. This will permit the strips to remain a constant width whatever the final diameter of the box becomes.

8 After the inlaid panels are complete and each panel is cut to length, shape the inside radius on the second armature block. Use 80 grit sandpaper on the surface and construct a mandrel from ¼ in threaded rod (it can also be used for the final sanding of the box before the armature webs are cut away (see diagram 6)). It is now easy to sand each panel to the exact shape to sit on the armature (see diagram 4).

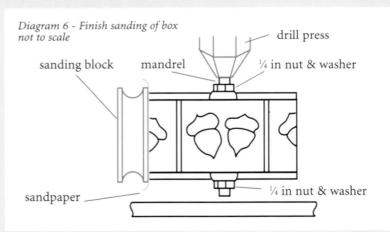

Diagram 6 - Finish sanding of box
not to scale

drill press

sanding block   mandrel   ¼ in nut & washer

sandpaper   ¼ in nut & washer

Shaped inlaid panel ready to fit on armature

The Art of Wood Inlay

9 Fitting inlaid panels to the armature requires little or no clamping. I used a rub fit. Thinly cover all surfaces with glue and rub the panel on the surface of the armature until you have wood-on-wood contact. The panel will adhere firmly to the armature (much like two panes of glass adhere to each other when water gets between them). Hold each panel in place with finger pressure for a minute for a perfect joint.

10 After the first panel is trimmed to the exact width (diagram 7) fit panel 2 to panel 1. Fit panel 3 to panel 2, then glue panel 2 to the armature and panel 1. Then fit panel 4 to panel 3. Adjust the angle on any of the partition strips as necessary. Any small adjustment needed to the angle on the sides of each panel is easily accomplished using the jig in diagram 7.

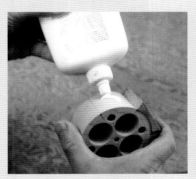
Glue panels to armature

Glue panels to armature

11 After all the panels are in place and the top and bottom edges have been sanded flush and square to the armature, turn the outside of the box round again (diagram 8) to define the outside dimension to the box.

12 Use a V fence on the router table and a ¼ in straight cut bit to define the inside dimension of the box (see diagrams 9 and 10). The depth and width of this cut are not exact. This removes some of the armature core in preparation to gluing on the box facings. Leave enough strength to the armature webbing to spin the box one more time (diagrams 9 and 10).

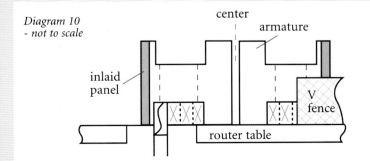
Diagram 10 - not to scale
center
armature
inlaid panel
V fence
router table

Diagram 7 - Sanding jig not to scale
disk sander

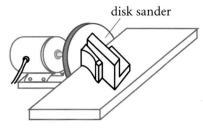

Diagram 8a -scale- half size

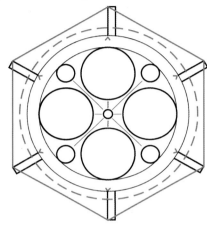

Diagram 8b -not to scale
¼ in drill bit
disk sander
jig   block

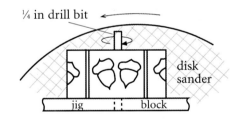

Diagram 9 -not to scale
router V fence
router table
¼ in router bit

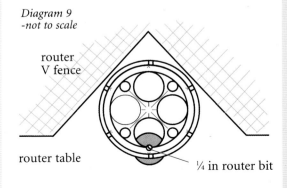

Round Acorn Box

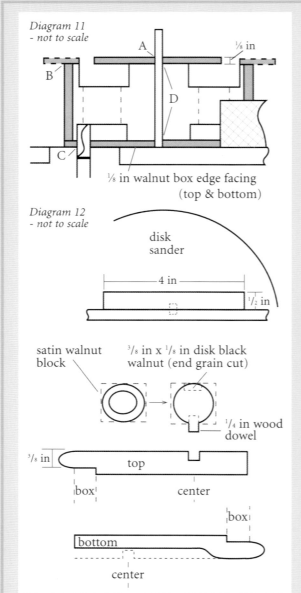

Diagram 11
- not to scale

A

⅛ in

B

D

C

⅛ in walnut box edge facing
(top & bottom)

Diagram 12
- not to scale

disk
sander

4 in

½ in

satin walnut
block

⅜ in x ⅛ in disk black
walnut (end grain cut)

¼ in wood
dowel

⅜ in

top

box

center

box

bottom

center

Construct your own sanding jig slightly smaller than the interior
dimension of the box & finish sanding the interior

Disk

13 The finished width of the edge of the box is ⁵⁄₁₆ in. The box edge facing is ⅛ in black walnut, the same material used for the partitions. Use two single pieces cut to sufficient length and width to cover the ends of the box.

14 Use a ¼ in drill bit to drill a ¼ in hole in the center of each square, diagram 11A.

15 Center each piece on the ends of the box, and glue and clamp the facing to the ends of the box. Lightly tack this facing piece to the center post of the armature with a small dab of glue (diagram 11D).

16 Use the jig block (diagram 2) to sand the facings flush with the edges of the box (diagram 11B). Trim the inside edges on the router table (diagram 11C). The small dab of glue holding the facing material to the center of the armature will prevent the center piece of the facing material from jamming the router bit after it has been cut free of the edge.

17 After removing the center facing material, place the box on the mandrel and finish sanding the inlay panels (diagram 6).

The webs of the armature can be cut free

18 The webs of the armature can now be cut free. Construct your own sanding jig slightly smaller than the interior dimension of the box to finish sanding the interior.

19 To construct box top and bottom (diagram 12) turn two disks 4 in diameter using a short ¼ in pivot point and sanding disk. Turn the disk round and cut their profile using the router and router table with a V fence.

20 Inlay a ⅜ in disk of end grain black walnut into the end grain of a small block of satin walnut. Turn the acorn top free hand. Use a short piece of ¼ in wood dowel to attach it to the box top.

The Art of Wood Inlay

Inlay Procedure

1 The inlay details for this project illustrate the construction of an acorn and acorn cap that are separated (same process used for end of branch detail for Recipe Box and Recipe Book Stand projects, p59). Added interest comes from 3 inlay segments with green acorns (tulip poplar), 3 from satin walnut, one with a separate acorn and cap. Cut caps for green acorns from end grain cuts of light mahogany. Cut brown acorn caps from dark mahogany.

2 After constructing acorn (see Trinket Box project) place it in position (see inlay procedure p14) and scribe around it as usual. Remove acorn and cut a shoulder to the scribed line.

3 Remove $1/16$ in of material from cavity to make clearly defined dimensional shape. To do this begin cutting the cavity using the largest drill bit that will fit within the shape or drill several small holes. The relief cut will allow the chisels to cut vertical edges cleanly.

4 Complete shaping the cavity using a set of small wood files.

Pattern-Acorn inlay - scale full size

*steps
scale - full size*

Scribe around the acorn for start of inlay process

Accent line with $1/8$ in round carving tool to cut small radius

Define size if incision

Wood choices - Acorns

■	Mahogany
■	Satin walnut
■	Black walnut

Drill to excavate the cavity to cut relief cut

Use chisel to finish cutting the verticals

Inlay cavity right through wood

Bevel bottom of inlay to place in inlay hole

Apply glue on acorn construct

Place glued acorn construct into hole

In vise press acorn construct into hole with two blocks

Acorn inlay

Round Acorn Box

Earrings, Brooches, Bracelet

The woods for this project are exotic. I prize the dark color and texture of the Ceylon ebony and the rich color of the ornamental plum root that was a gift from my neighbor. I have used these special pieces to highlight many projects over the years. The challenge for this project was to find the best way to work with the ebony so it would not discolor the plum root when finishing the pieces.

Note   Project uses basic inlay techniques

Base Material & Inlay Material
Ceylon ebony, ornamental plum, hard maple

Bracelet Construction

1 Use the same construction procedure as for the Round Acorn Box project (p84).
2 Using dimensions shown in diagram 1 (p92), construct an armature of hard maple.
3 The internal finished dimension of this bracelet is 2³/₄ in. Be sure to turn the armature large enough to allow an armature wall ¹/₈ in thick.
4 Divide the circumference of the armature into 8 equal segments. The R dimension is equal to half the diagonal of a square drawn equal to the diameter of the armature.
5 Secure facings to bracelet and trim their inside and outside dimensions.
6 The final finishing is now done with a scraper because sanding will make the ebony bleed into almost any other wood. A wide very sharp chisel works well.

Earrings, Brooches Construction

1 Prepare inlay pieces for earrings and brooches. Use a bench hook (diagram 3) to support base block of ebony in order to carve out inlay cavities. This will also give support when you plane inlay flush. Cut the bench hook from a single piece of wood or glue on end blocks. Do not use nails or screws.
2 Scribe around secured inlay pieces which has been tacked to the base block with a dab of glue. Do not use primary bevel on inlay piece. Carve out cavity to depth of half the thickness of the final piece.
3 Apply small secondary bevel to inlay piece before pressing into cavity. Glue and plane flush. Since the base block was small I did not cut it to the desired thickness until the inlay was pressed into place and trimmed flush. Placing these inlays into a thicker block lessens the chance that the block will split if the inlay is too tight. It helps to inlay pieces slightly off the direction of the grain of the base block.
4 I used the same edge treatment for the brooches as I did for the bracelet. Brooches are ¹/₈ in round over on both sides. The edges of the earrings are beveled by hand in a pitch block (see diagram 4).
5 Purchase fittings of your choice and glue them on.

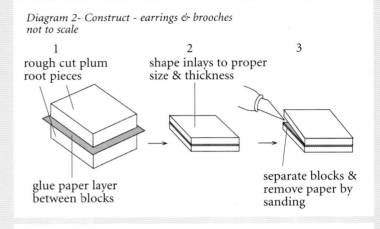

Diagram 2- Construct - earrings & brooches not to scale

1 rough cut plum root pieces
2 shape inlays to proper size & thickness
3

glue paper layer between blocks

separate blocks & remove paper by sanding

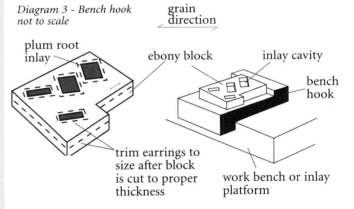

Diagram 3 - Bench hook not to scale

grain direction

plum root inlay

ebony block

inlay cavity

bench hook

trim earrings to size after block is cut to proper thickness

work bench or inlay platform

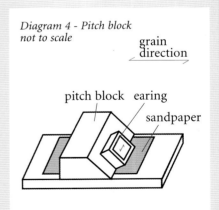

Diagram 4 - Pitch block not to scale

grain direction

pitch block   earing

sandpaper

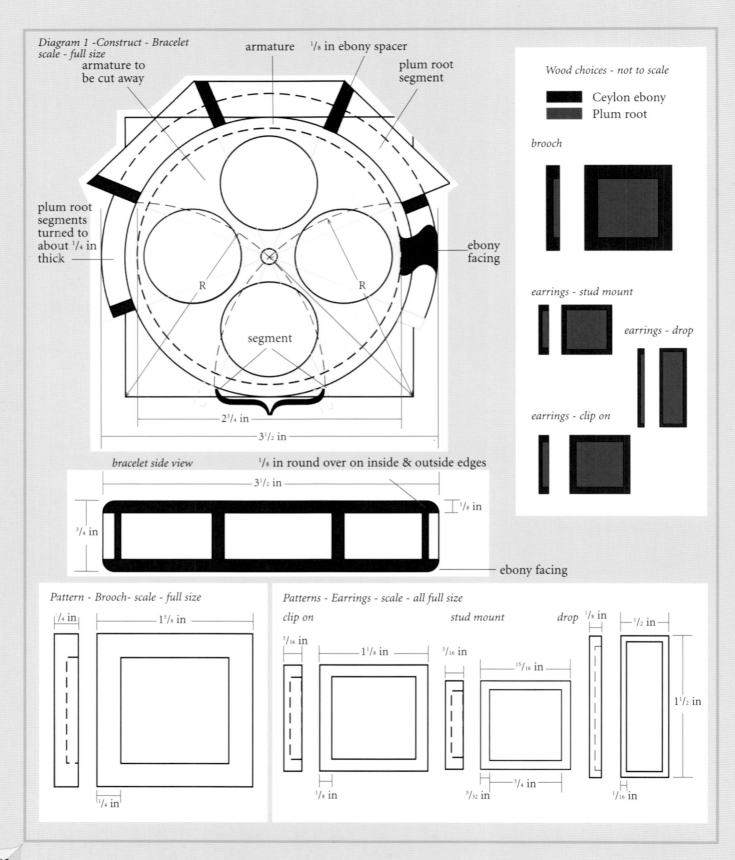

Diagram 1 -Construct - Bracelet scale - full size

armature

armature to be cut away

¹/₈ in ebony spacer

plum root segment

plum root segments turned to about ¹/₄ in thick

ebony facing

R

R

segment

2³/₄ in

3¹/₂ in

Wood choices - not to scale

Ceylon ebony
Plum root

brooch

earrings - stud mount

earrings - drop

earrings - clip on

bracelet side view

¹/₈ in round over on inside & outside edges

3¹/₂ in

³/₄ in

¹/₈ in

ebony facing

Pattern - Brooch- scale - full size

¹/₄ in

1⁵/₈ in

¹/₄ in

Patterns - Earrings - scale - all full size

clip on

stud mount

drop

¹/₈ in

¹/₂ in

³/₁₆ in

1¹/₈ in

³/₁₆ in

¹/₈ in

¹⁵/₁₆ in

³/₃₂ in

³/₄ in

1¹/₂ in

¹/₁₆ in

Walnut Tulip Plaque

This inlay is presented in shades of walnut that blend with the background wood to achieve a soft picture. It would not be difficult to draw this tulip in several poses and inlay several complementary tiles to enhance any other project such as cabinet doors or furniture. Using different woods could also make this a very colorful project.

Base Material

Black walnut 11⁵/₈ in x 6 in x ³/₈ in

Maple strips ¹/₄ in x ¹/₄ in

Inlay Material

Black walnut - various shades

Frame Construction

1 The ¹/₄ in x ¹/₄ in maple strips should be inlaid into the frame side and end rails before cutting the rabbets to hold the tile (see diagram 2, detail A). I used a ¹/₄ in straight cut router bit in my table-mounted router. After the glue has set and the frame material is again sanded to the finished dimension the rabbets can be cut in the frame pieces (see note B).
2 To cut the end rails into the side rails see note C. Use the inlay technique (p14). Size each mortise, which will accept the end of a top or bottom rail, by placing the end of the piece in position on the side rail and scribe around it, as if it were an inlay piece.
3 Remove the rail and cut a shoulder with the inlay knife. Using a sharp chisel and mallet cut the mortise the exact size of the rail making a perfect joint.
4 The inlaid walnut tile should fit in the frame with about ¹/₁₆ in clearance from the side rail to allow for any expansion of the wood due to any increase in humidity. This is not generally a problem in such small pieces of wood. However, relocation from living in a dry desert area to moist tropical one will always be problematic to any wood items.
5 Secure the inlay tile in the frame by placing a small amount of glue in the frame at four points (center point of each rail) around the tile. Cut hanger in back of tile (see p27).

Inlay Procedure

1 Transfer (p12) inlay parts pattern to inlay wood. Cut out. Proceed with inlay steps, p14.
2 Constructing tulip leaves before they are inlaid can be time consuming. Inlay each half of the leaf separately (using overlay techniques).

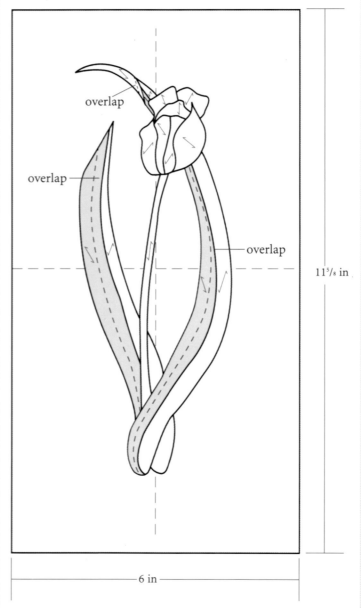

Diagram 1A -Pattern - Walnut Tulip Plaque
scale - half size
Note - diagram 1B on p96

grain
direction

inlaid tile ³/₈ in thick black walnut
inlay material different shades of black walnut

overlap

overlap

overlap

11⁵/₈ in

6 in

Diagram 2- Detail -Frame construction
scale - full size

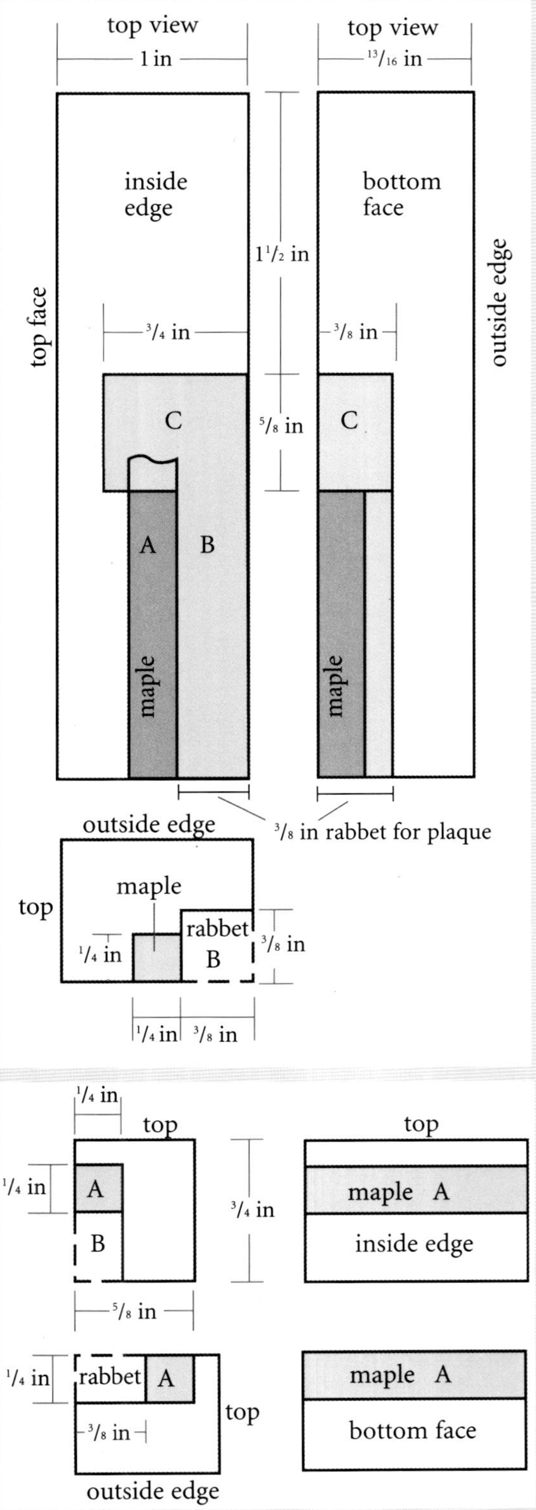

top view
1 in
top view
13/16 in
inside
edge
bottom
face
top face
outside edge
1 1/2 in
3/4 in
3/8 in
5/8 in
C
C
A
B
maple
maple
outside edge
3/8 in rabbet for plaque
maple
top
rabbet
B
1/4 in
3/8 in
1/4 in
3/8 in
1/4 in
top
1/4 in
A
B
3/4 in
5/8 in
top
maple A
inside edge
1/4 in
rabbet
A
top
3/8 in
outside edge
maple A
bottom face

Diagram 2 - Frame construction
scale - half size

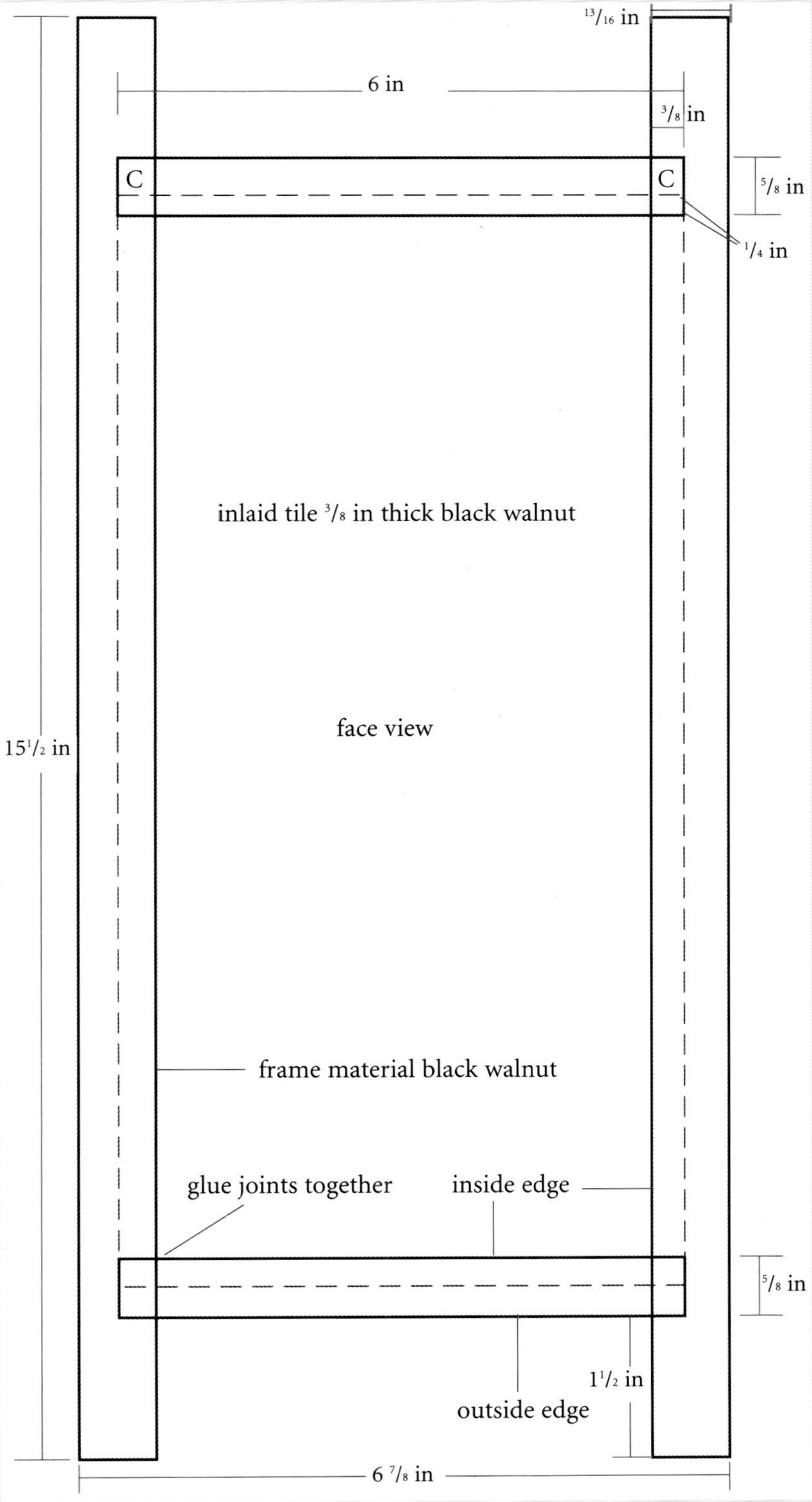

13/16 in
6 in
3/8 in
C
C
5/8 in
1/4 in
inlaid tile 3/8 in thick black walnut
face view
15 1/2 in
frame material black walnut
glue joints together
inside edge
5/8 in
1 1/2 in
outside edge
6 7/8 in

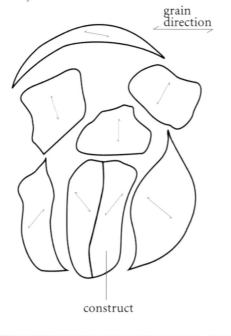

Diagram 1 B - Pattern - Tulip flower head scale - full size

grain direction

construct

Note   Project uses constructs & lap inlay techniques

Diagram 3 - steps - not to scale

step 1

step 2

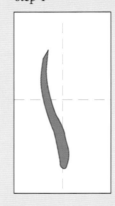

step 3

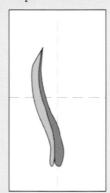

step 4

step 5

step 6

step 7

step 8

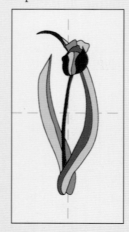

Wood choices - Walnut Tulip Plaque

- Black walnut
- Black walnut (different shade)
- Black walnut (different shade)
- Black walnut (different shade)
- Black walnut (different shade)

Yellow Rose Plaque

I used two pieces of amarillo for the rose petals. The two different shades make highlighted areas that look like reflected light with shadows.

Base Material
American black walnut 15¼ in x 11 in x ¼ in
Plywood for template

Inlay Material
Amarillo (roses), tulip poplar (leaves), crystobal (stems of thorns), birch (end of stem detail)

Base Construction

1 Make oval shape template for rose plaque from ¼ in plywood according to diagram 1. See diagram of ellipse poinsettia p47. Ovals of different sizes can be made by changing the router base plate. Make 2 perimeter cuts to establish the inner dimension of the plaque. If using ¼ in router, make each pass ⅛ in deep to reach a depth of ⅜ in.

2 Remove remainder of material from center of plaque in the same way as described for the Lazy Susan project p53.

3 Round over outside bottom edge of plaque with ¾ in round over bit (see diagram 2A).

4 See plaque hanging method to hang plaque flat to the wall (see diagram 2B). It requires no other fixture and can be used for all wall hangings.

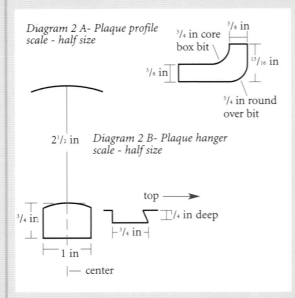

Diagram 2 A- Plaque profile scale - half size

¾ in core box bit
⅜ in
13/16 in
⅜ in
¾ in round over bit

2½ in *Diagram 2 B- Plaque hanger scale - half size*

top →
¾ in
¼ in deep
¾ in
1 in
center

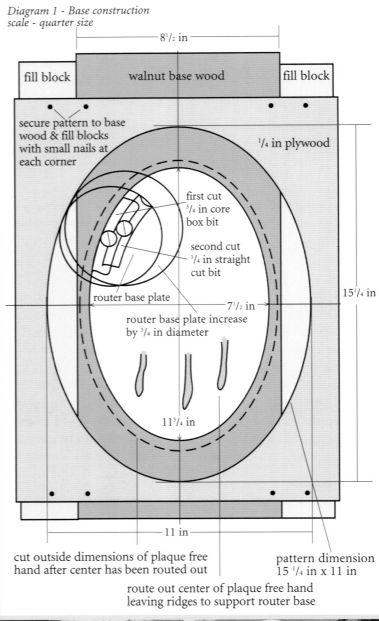

Diagram 1 - Base construction scale - quarter size

8½ in

fill block   walnut base wood   fill block

secure pattern to base wood & fill blocks with small nails at each corner

¼ in plywood

first cut ¾ in core box bit

second cut ¾ in straight cut bit

router base plate

router base plate increase by ¾ in diameter

15¼ in

7½ in

11¾ in

11 in

pattern dimension 15 ¼ in x 11 in

cut outside dimensions of plaque free hand after center has been routed out

route out center of plaque free hand leaving ridges to support router base

Plywood template

Addition of ⅜ in ring to router base plate

Inlay Procedure

1 Using master pattern create transparency print of each petal piece.

2 Use transparency prints to select grain direction and mark out each petal piece on inlay material. Use carbon paper to trace shape onto inlay wood (photo 3).

3 Cut out petal pieces on scroll saw (photo 4).

4 Adjust size and shape on crow's foot with small wood files (photo 5).

5 Using reference marks, accurately place master print on base wood. Using carbon paper transfer just enough information to base wood to locate first inlay piece (do not trace entire outline of piece).

6 Secure inlay piece with dab of glue.

7 Follow inlay procedure p14.

8 Inlay entire picture using master print to locate each inlay piece in order given.

9 See p100 for inlay order for stems of leaves. The calyx leaves on steps 5, 6, 9, 10, 12, 14 will have ends overlaid.

Note   When constructing these rose heads some pieces can be assembled and inlaid as constructs, or they may all be inlaid separately.

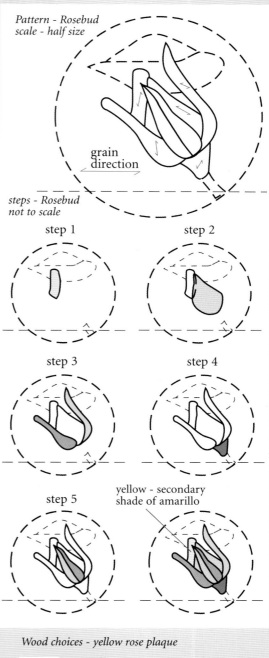

Pattern - Rosebud
scale - half size

grain direction

steps - Rosebud
not to scale

step 1   step 2

step 3   step 4

step 5   yellow - secondary shade of amarillo

Wood choices - yellow rose plaque

	Amarillo
	Amarillo (different shade)
	Crystobal
	Crystobal (different shade)
	Birch (end grain cut)
	Tulip poplar
	Tulip poplar (different shade)
	Tulip poplar (different shade)

1 Green & yellow streaked amarillo

2 Master print pattern

3 Use transparency to mark petal pattern on wood

4 Cutting petal parts on scroll saw

Note   Project uses constructs, overlay & lap inlay techniques

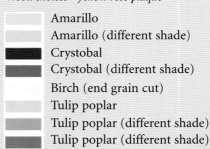

5 Size & shape with wood file

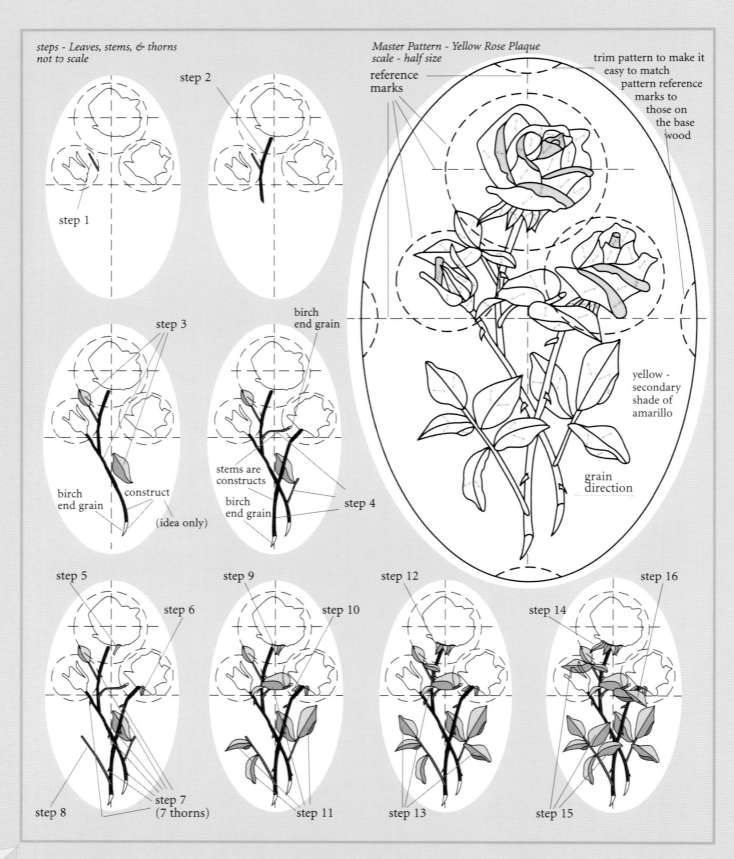

steps - Leaves, stems, & thorns
not to scale

step 2

step 1

Master Pattern - Yellow Rose Plaque
scale - half size

reference
marks

trim pattern to make it
easy to match
pattern reference
marks to
those on
the base
wood

step 3

birch
end grain

birch
end grain

construct

(idea only)

stems are
constructs

birch
end grain

step 4

yellow -
secondary
shade of
amarillo

grain
direction

step 5

step 6

step 9

step 10

step 12

step 16

step 14

step 8

step 7
(7 thorns)

step 11

step 13

step 15

The Art of Wood Inlay

Pattern - Medium size rose
scale - full size

grain
direction

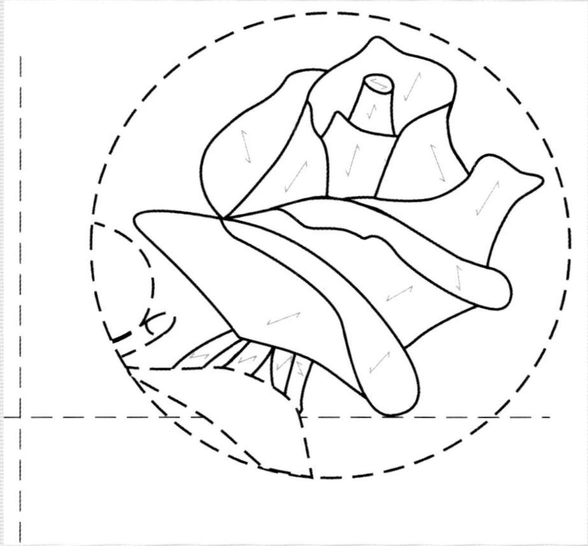

yellow - secondary
shade of amarillo

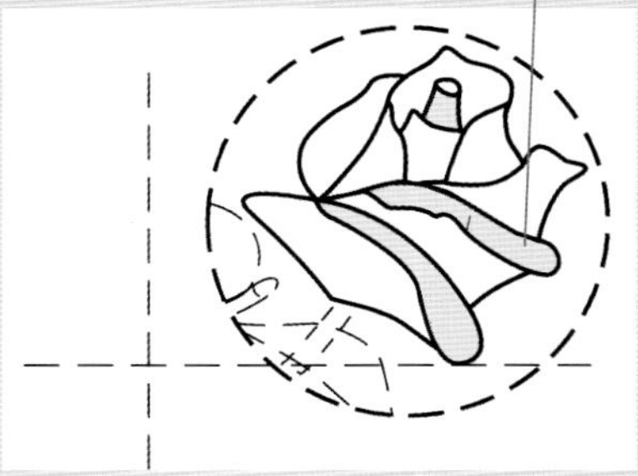

steps for medium size rose
not to scale

construct

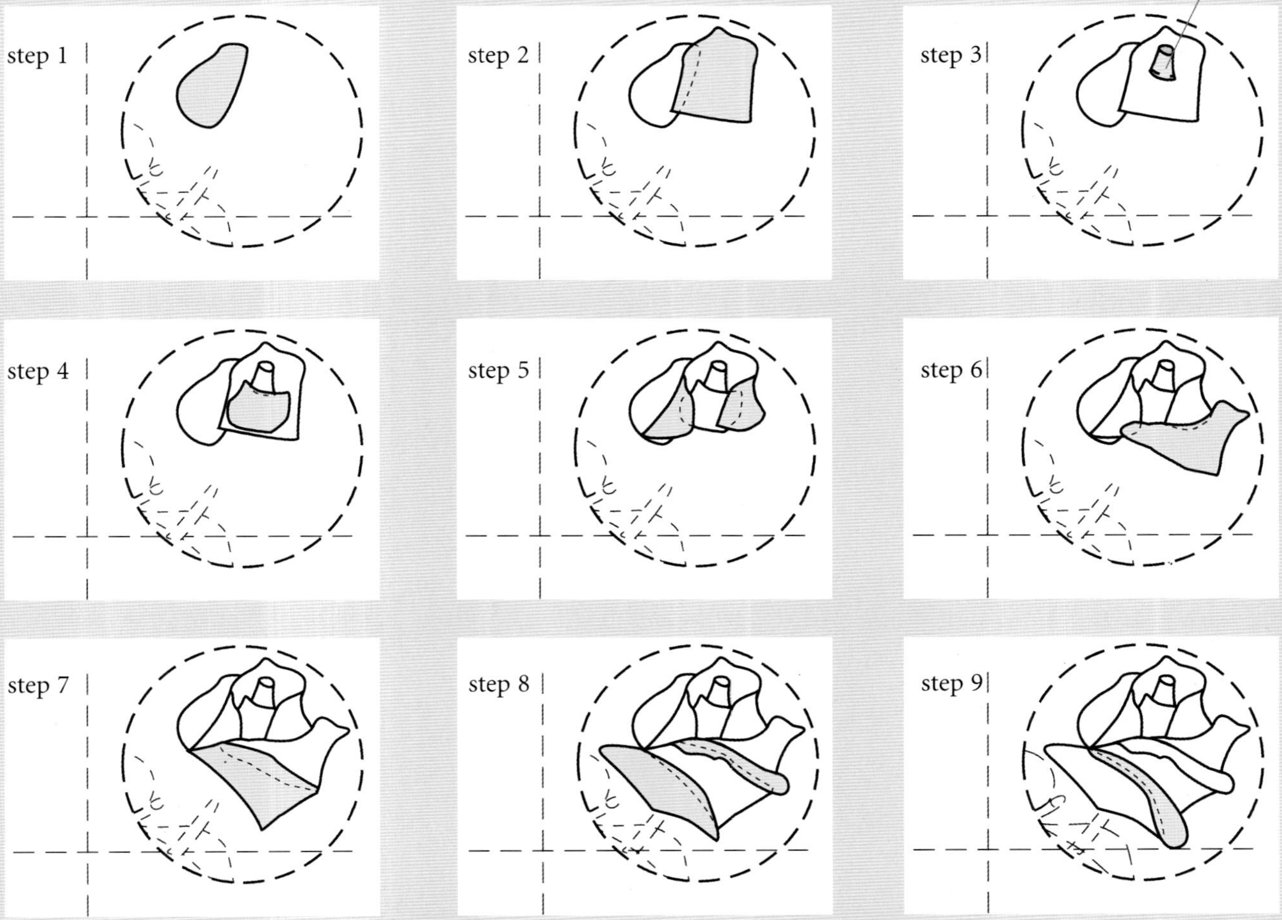

step 1

step 2

step 3

step 4

step 5

step 6

step 7

step 8

step 9

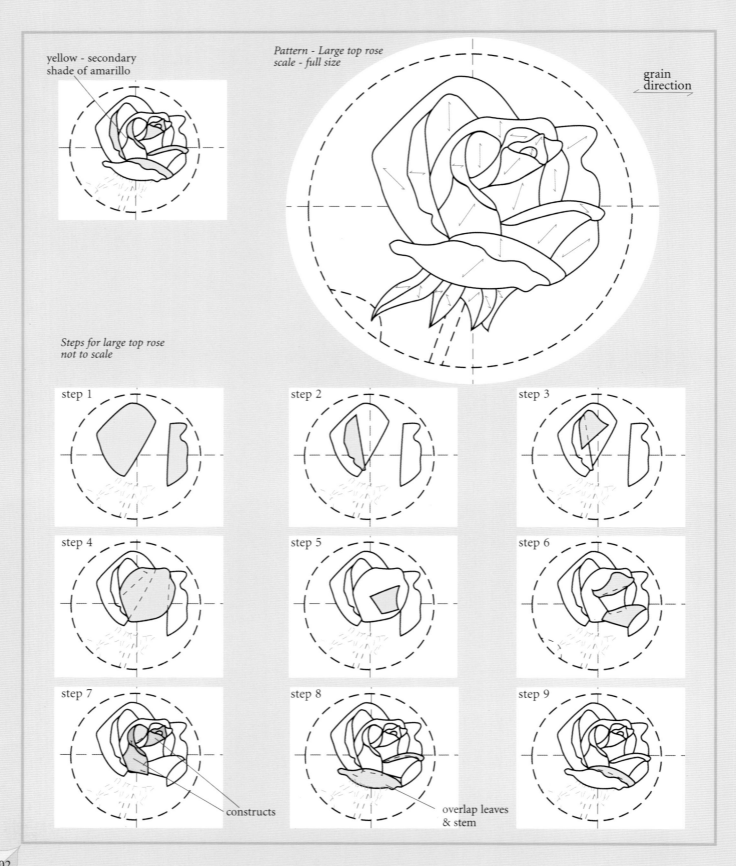

yellow - secondary
shade of amarillo

Pattern - Large top rose
scale - full size

grain
direction

Steps for large top rose
not to scale

step 1

step 2

step 3

step 4

step 5

step 6

step 7

step 8

step 9

constructs

overlap leaves
& stem

The Art of Wood Inlay

Pin Tray

This pin tray was carved from a single piece of cocobolo. The inlay copies a piece of jewelry that has special memories.

Base Material
Cocobolo 1 in x 6 in x 12 in
Inlay Material
Bloodwood (flower), purpleheart (flower), amarillo (flower center, end grain cut), caragana (wrap wood), Russian olive (stems)

Tray Construction

1 See diagrams 1 and 2 for tray dimensions. Cut the interior of the tray from base wood. Define the inside edges with ¾ in core box router bit (diagram 3, detail A). Use router mounted in router table and a straight fence to control the wood blank. Continue to remove remainder of material with a straight cut bit (see detail B). Cutting the inside of the tray first allows you to adjust inside dimension larger if you don't achieve a clean edge on the first try.

2 Using a drill press and a Forstner style wood bit define the external profile of the tray corners and the inside corners of the handles (see detail C).

3 Using ¾ in core box router bit cut 2 channels across the ends of the tray on the bottom side to create profile on underside of handle (see detail D).

4 With a saw cut in from each end of tray to remove waste material (see detail E).

5 Remove remainder of material inside handle (see detail F).

6 Cut out tray to final outside dimensions.

7 Complete inlays at this point (see wrapped inlay process this page).

8 Carve out leg profiles with ¾ in core box router bit mounted in router table, using a straight fence (see detail G in diagram 3).

9 Remove remainder of waste material from bottom of tray using straight cut router bit (see detail H).

10 Where possible, finish all corners (edges) of the tray by using ⅛ in round over router bit with guide bearing mounted in the router table. Other edges are rounded over by hand using sandpaper. Use drum sanders mounted in a drill press to sand handle cutouts and inside corners.

Inlay procedure for petal inlays

Planing shavings from caragana wood

Thick shavings ready for wrapped inlay

Rough inlay material for petals glued to make leaf

Inlay material trimmed to proper thickness

2 petals drawn on this inlay construct

Petals cut out

Wrap petals with caragana & glue

Petal construct ready to be inlaid & inlaid wrapped petals

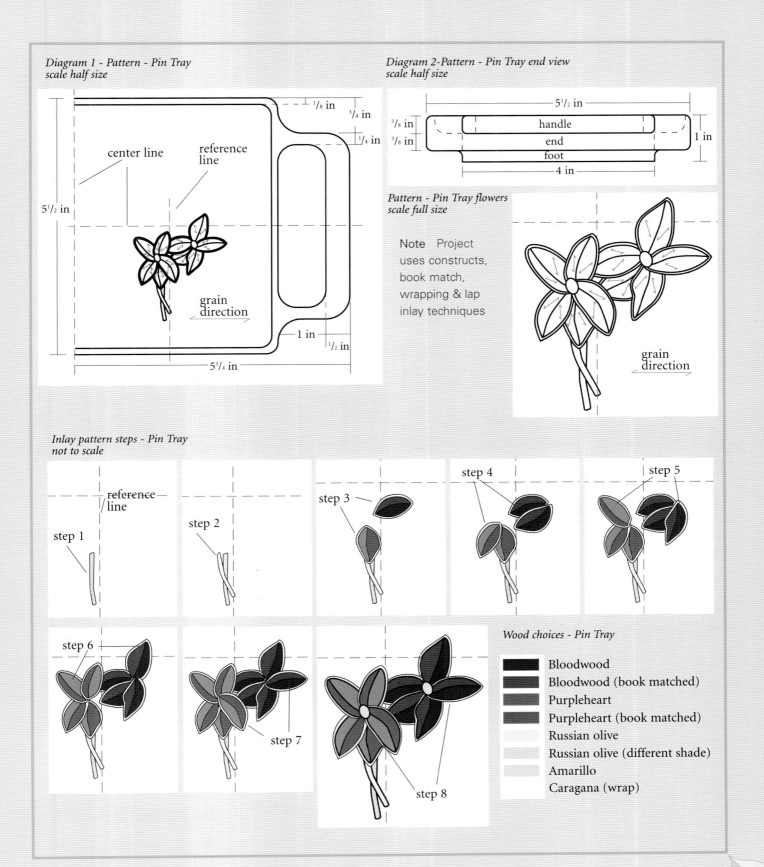

Diagram 1 - Pattern - Pin Tray
scale half size

center line   reference line

5¹/₂ in

grain direction

5³/₄ in

1 in
¹/₈ in
³/₄ in
¹/₄ in
¹/₂ in

Diagram 2-Pattern - Pin Tray end view
scale half size

5¹/₂ in
³/₈ in
³/₈ in
handle
end
foot
1 in
4 in

Pattern - Pin Tray flowers
scale full size

Note   Project uses constructs, book match, wrapping & lap inlay techniques

grain direction

Inlay pattern steps - Pin Tray
not to scale

reference line

step 1
step 2
step 3
step 4
step 5
step 6
step 7
step 8

Wood choices - Pin Tray

Bloodwood
Bloodwood (book matched)
Purpleheart
Purpleheart (book matched)
Russian olive
Russian olive (different shade)
Amarillo
Caragana (wrap)

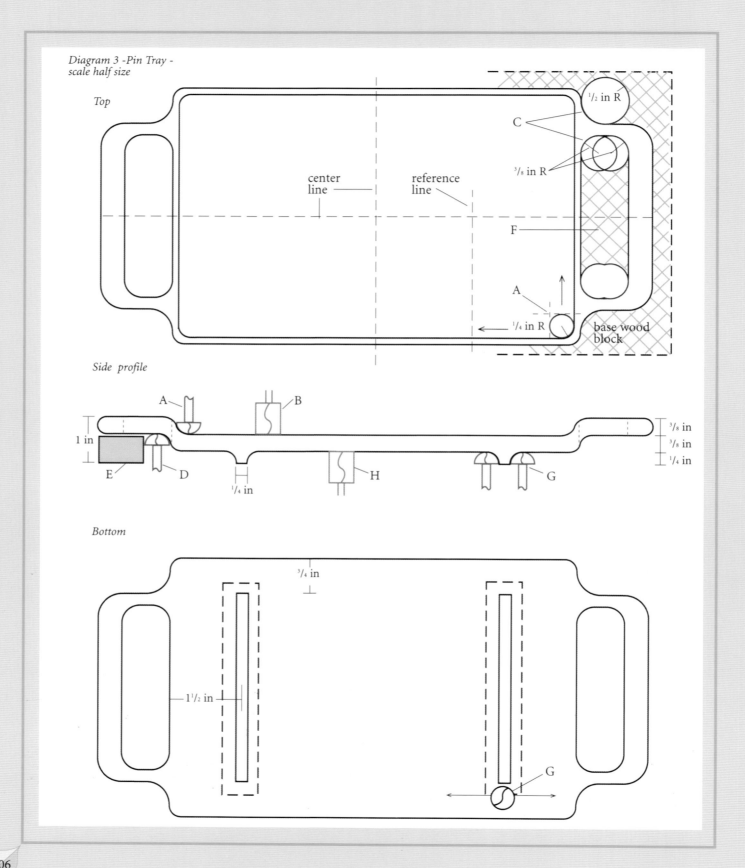

*Diagram 3 -Pin Tray -
scale half size*

Top

¹/₂ in R

C

³/₈ in R

center
line

reference
line

F

A

¹/₄ in R

base wood
block

Side profile

A

B

³/₈ in

³/₈ in

¹/₄ in

1 in

E

D

¹/₄ in

H

G

Bottom

³/₄ in

1¹/₂ in

G

Christmas Ornaments

These four Christmas ornaments have the same base and all can be made at one time. Make one or two extras so that you can set up your machines and adjust your jigs with one of the extra pieces. The other one can be a spare to replace a piece you may destroy while working with it. This project is quite difficult.

Base Material (one ornament)
American cherry 5½ in x 4 in x ½ in
Inlay Material
Poinsettia   Manitoba maple (flower petals), tulip poplar (green leaves), amarillo (center detail)
Holly leaves   Tulip poplar, holly, pernambuco
Spruce tree   Tulip poplar, holly, moradillo
Candle   Caragana, bloodwood, moradillo, tulip poplar, amarillo, pernambuco, purpleheart, Ceylon ebony, American cherry

Base Construction
1 Draw pattern (p109) of ornament onto base wood (see diagram 1).
2 Cut to shape with scroll saw ¹⁄₁₆ in oversize.
3 Drill ³⁄₃₂ in hole in center of handle.
4 Drill ¼ in pivot point ¼ in deep in center of ornament.
5 True up size of each ornament using following instructions:
   a Construct a base platform (see diagram 2).
   b Using ³⁄₃₂ in drill bit as pivot point in platform jig, advance the platform jig forward to engage ornament base into sanding drum. Secure jig with clamps.
   c Rotate ornament against rotating sanding drum to true radius of handle. Advance platform jig in small steps until desired radius is obtained.
   d Using ¼ in pivot point raised ¼ in from platform jig, repeat the operation to true the dimension of larger radius of ornament. Construct pivot point from a short piece of ¼ in hardwood dowel or piece of ¼ in drill bit ground off to a convenient length. Using freehand techniques, sand neck profile against sanding drum.
6 Route out the center of ornaments using the following instructions:
   a Construct a jig similar to the one used for the drill press (see diagram 3).
   b Clamp jig to router table so ³⁄₁₆ in core box router bit will cut the desired radius.
   c Set depth of router to ¼ in (half the thickness of the base wood).
   d Starting the router, hold the ornament base firmly in hand in the position shown in diagram 4, with the center line of the ornament aligned with the center line marked on the jig. Lower ornament onto the pivot point slowly allowing ornament to engage router bit. When the base is flat on the jig, smoothly rotate ornament clockwise on router bit while firmly holding the ornament base down on the center pivot. After completing this cut,

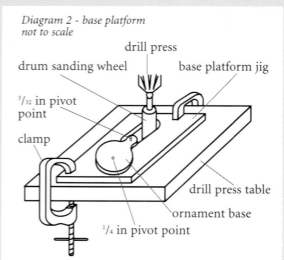

Diagram 2 - base platform
not to scale

drill press
drum sanding wheel
base platform jig
³⁄₃₂ in pivot point
clamp
drill press table
ornament base
¼ in pivot point

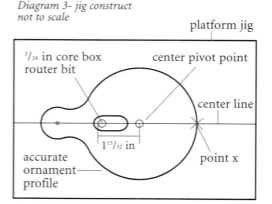

Diagram 3- jig construct
not to scale

platform jig
³⁄₁₆ in core box router bit
center pivot point
center line
1¹⁵⁄₃₂ in
accurate ornament profile
point x

slot in platform jig to allow jig to be set for different radius cuts

Diagram 4 - Christmas Ornaments router setting
not to scale

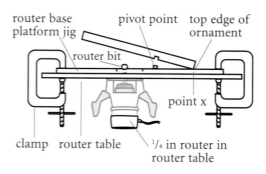

router base platform jig
pivot point
top edge of ornament
router bit
point x
clamp   router table
¼ in router in router table

turn router off and remove ornament (operation is easier if router is operated with a foot switch).

e Replace ³⁄₁₆ in core box bit with ½ in straight bit. Using same method as above, make a radius cut 1³⁄₁₆ in outside diameter to ¼ in (or slightly less).

f Make a third radius cut to remove material, as shown in diagram 5.

g Remove rest of material in center of base freehand, passing the base back and forth over the router bit. Add outside edge profile after inlay is complete. This allows placing each base into a jig (that is secured with cleats over the edge of the inlay platform) cut to the ornament's profile. The jig helps to hold each piece while doing the inlay. The outside edge is done with a ³⁄₁₆ in round over router bit set to a depth to leave ¹⁄₁₆ in shoulder profile on each side.

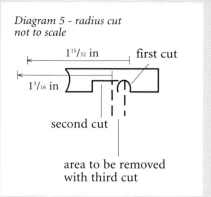

Diagram 5 - radius cut
not to scale

$1^{15}/_{32}$ in — first cut

$1^{3}/_{16}$ in

second cut

area to be removed
with third cut

Diagram 1 - Christmas ornament construct
scale - full size

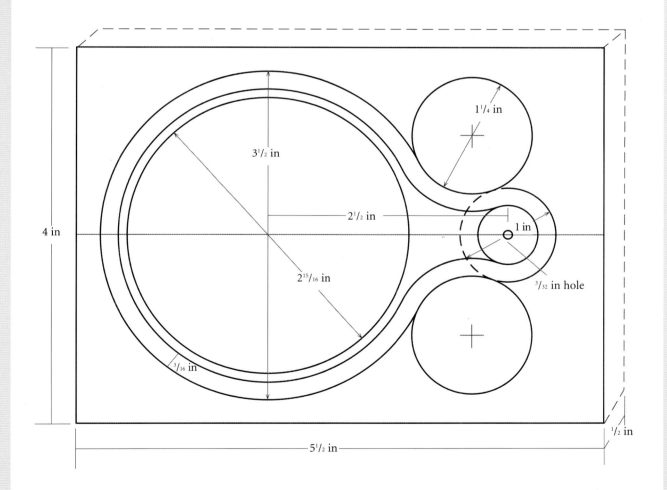

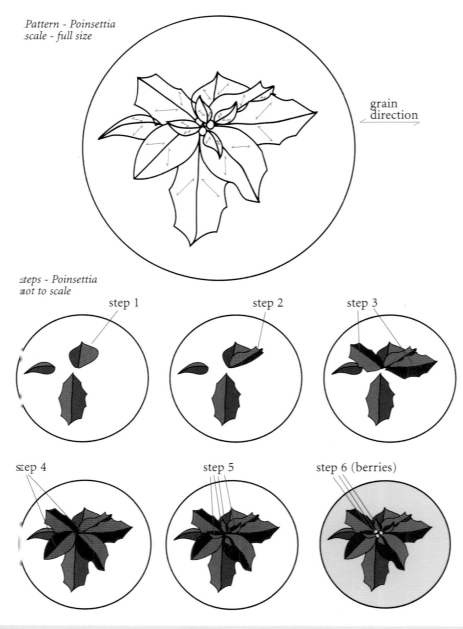

Pattern - Poinsettia
scale - full size

grain direction

Steps - Poinsettia
not to scale

step 1

step 2

step 3

step 4

step 5

step 6 (berries)

Wood choices - Poinsettia

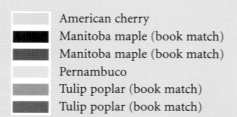

American cherry
Manitoba maple (book match)
Manitoba maple (book match)
Pernambuco
Tulip poplar (book match)
Tulip poplar (book match)

Inlay Procedure
Poinsettia Inlay

1 Inlaying this piece is a straight-forward overlap, one petal over the other. Start with the leaves, then proceed with the lower underling petals, then with the smaller inner petals on top, then the center detail. All the leaves and petals are constructed book match (p16). See pattern this page and follow inlay techniques outlined on p14. Center detail is made from end grain cuts of amarillo.

Holly Leaves Inlay

1 The technique here is double inlay. Using pattern (p12) cut and book match (p16) the holly leaves (see procedure p14).
2 Inlay finished leaves into a block of holly wood. Allow 12 hours for glue to set completely.
3 Rip holly block to the thickness of inlay material.
4 With a scroll saw, recut the leaves, leaving a thin white border around them.
5 Using a crow's foot and a small half round file, file the edges of the border of the leaf to an even width.
6 Inlay the finished leaves into the ornament.
7 Make the berries from pernambuco

Note Project uses constructs, book match, lapping, double inlay & 2-stage inlay techniques

The Art of Wood Inlay

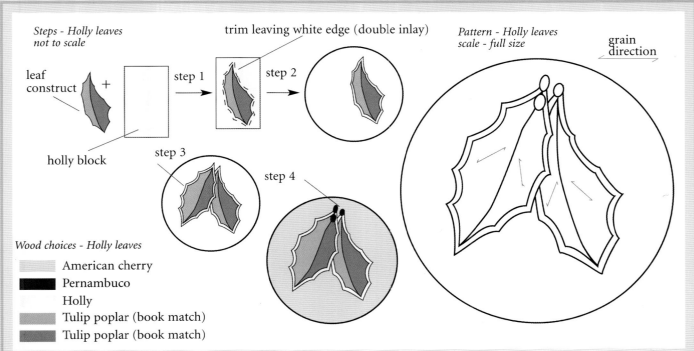

Steps - Holly leaves not to scale

trim leaving white edge (double inlay)

Pattern - Holly leaves scale - full size

grain direction

leaf construct + holly block → step 1 → step 2

step 3

step 4

Wood choices - Holly leaves

- American cherry
- Pernambuco
- Holly
- Tulip poplar (book match)
- Tulip poplar (book match)

Spruce Tree Inlay

1. Use the same inlay technique as for holly leaves.
2. Book match (p16) the tulip poplar, including in the construct a small sliver of moradillo for the tree trunk (pattern this page), making sure the angle of the grain in the poplar is pointing downward.
3. Mark a second line slightly smaller carving off that portion which you would like to highlight with snow.
4. Cut a profile of the tree, then inlay tree profile into a block of holly wood.
5. Allow glue to cure completely.
6. Rip holly block to proper inlay thickness and recut profile of tree (include the snow drift piece).
7. Inlay entire construct as one piece or snowdrift could be inlaid separately.

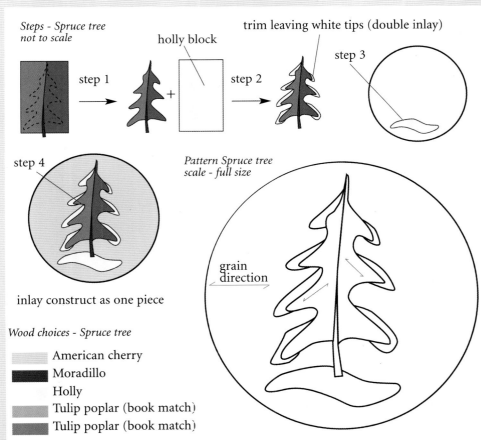

Steps - Spruce tree not to scale

holly block

trim leaving white tips (double inlay)

step 1 → + → step 2

step 3

step 4

inlay construct as one piece

Pattern Spruce tree scale - full size

grain direction

Wood choices - Spruce tree

- American cherry
- Moradillo
- Holly
- Tulip poplar (book match)
- Tulip poplar (book match)

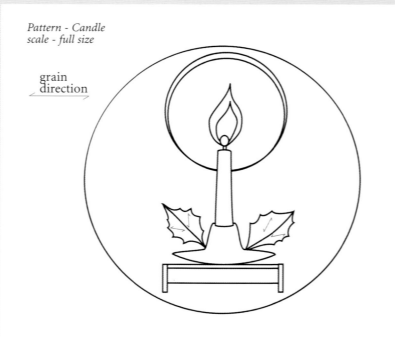

Pattern - Candle
scale - full size

grain
direction

Note Using a common wood (pine or birch, spruce) as the base wood you need only small pieces of the more expensive wood to put together a construct. Begin inlaying into the base wood a small piece of amarillo about the size of the flame. When this has firmly set, overlay the orange piece of the flame. Again, when firmly set, inlay a piece of purpleheart to make up the base of the flame. This piece can be slightly larger than the small amount to be used at the base of the flame (see diagram of candle flame construction). After all pieces have set cut out the profile of the finished candle flame and properly dress the finished construct to about ⅛ in (half the thickness of the base). This is a 2-stage inlay procedure.

Candle Inlay

1. Cut round disk of American cherry from same wood plank used for base to match as closely as possible the grain of the base.
2. Roughly cut the disk ⅜ in thick and true up the circle on a jig on a disk sanding wheel. Slowly by hand spin the disk mounted on a pivot point against the sanding disk until the desired size is attained.
3. Cut to proper inlay thickness (⅛ in thick, which is ½ the thickness of the routered section of the base).
4. Cut out a thin strip of caragana and wrap it around the disk (presoak the strip in hot tap water for about 5 minutes).
5. Secure with glue, using a flexible strap clamp made from a piece of light cardboard waxed and securely pinched on one side.
6. When dry, sand the strip of caragana freehand against the sanding disk to the desired thickness and shape. Taper it on the sides and completely sand it away on the bottom third of the disk.
7. Inlay disk into ornament.
8. Candle sits on a platform that is also a construct.
9. Glue thin strips of caragana to the sides of a small strip of bloodwood. Inlay as one piece.
10. Cut and shape candle holder from a piece of dark colored moradillo.
11. The candle is a piece of pernambuco. The wick is a small sliver of Ceylon ebony.
12. Place candle holder and candle on the base to locate wick. Inlay wick first. Inlay candle second, overlapping the bottom of the wick and making sure that the bottom of the candle will be below the top of the candle holder. When the candle holder is inlaid it will overlap the base of the candle leaving the best possible junction.
13. Make and inlay two small holly leaves from tulip poplar, as shown p113.
14. Make a construct for the flame. Make the orange section of flame from a piece of pernambuco and the base of the flame from a piece of purpleheart (see note).
15. Inlay into ornament and sand flush.

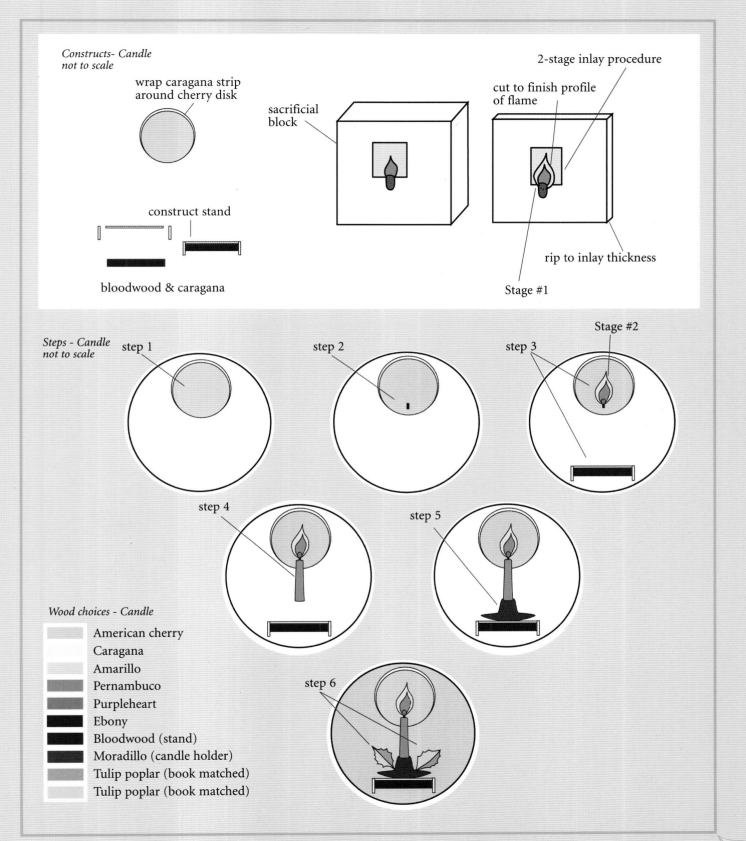

Constructs- Candle
not to scale

wrap caragana strip
around cherry disk

2-stage inlay procedure

cut to finish profile
of flame

sacrificial
block

construct stand

rip to inlay thickness

Stage #1

bloodwood & caragana

Steps - Candle
not to scale

step 1

step 2

step 3

Stage #2

step 4

step 5

step 6

Wood choices - Candle

American cherry
Caragana
Amarillo
Pernambuco
Purpleheart
Ebony
Bloodwood (stand)
Moradillo (candle holder)
Tulip poplar (book matched)
Tulip poplar (book matched)

Lily Bed Tray

This may seem to be a very difficult project to undertake, but by approaching it in two stages it is much simpler than it seems.

Base Material
Mahogany two pieces ³/₄ in thick

Inlay Material
Black walnut, amarillo, caragana, Ceylon ebony, tulip poplar, pao rosa, osage orange

Tray Construction

1 The base board for this bed tray is constructed from two pieces of ³/₄ in material glued together to achieve the desired tray width. It is planed to a thickness of ⁵/₈ in mainly to reduce the overall physical weight of the project.

2 Do not glue tray base board into frame. This is to allow for any swelling or shrinkage. The two blocks glued to the underside of the tray to support the folded legs will not pose any serious problems.

3 It is difficult to find ¹/₄ in x 2 in brass carriage bolts. My solution was to have the bolts brass plated. Cost was minimal.

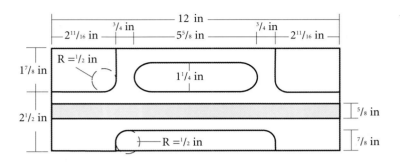

Diagram 1- end view
scale - quarter size

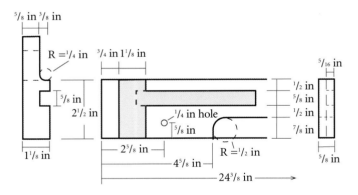

Diagram 2 - handle cutout
scale - quarter size

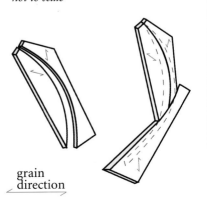

Diagram 4 - lily petal construct
not to scale

grain
direction

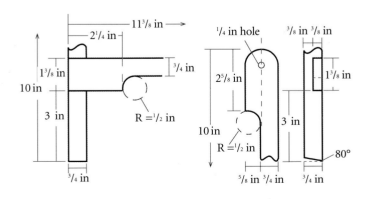

Diagram 3 - legs
scale - quarter size

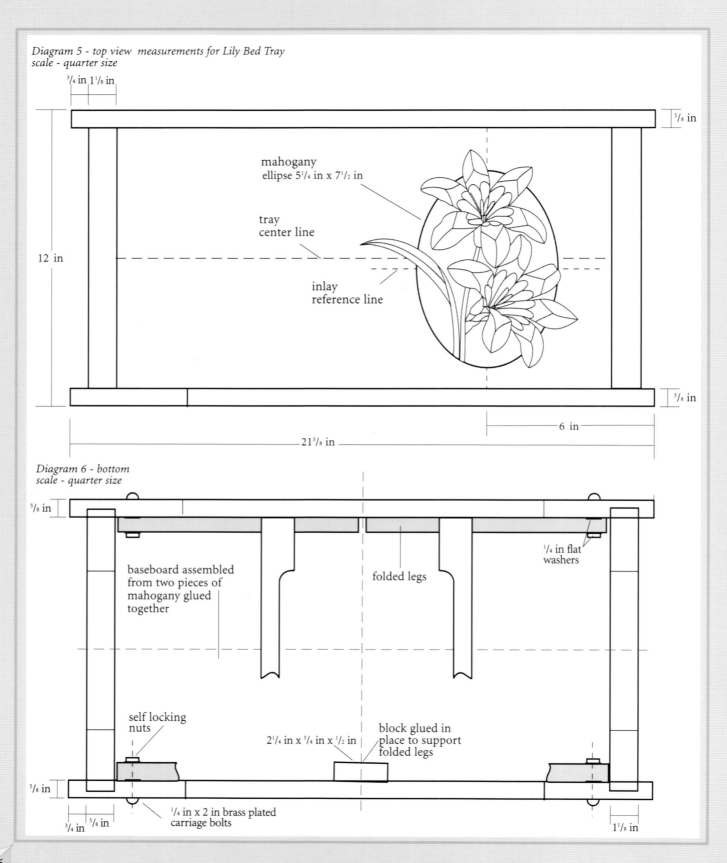

Diagram 5 - top view measurements for Lily Bed Tray
scale - quarter size

³/₄ in   1¹/₈ in

⁵/₈ in

mahogany
ellipse 5¹/₄ in x 7¹/₂ in

tray
center line

12 in

inlay
reference line

⁵/₈ in

6 in

21³/₈ in

Diagram 6 - bottom
scale - quarter size

⁵/₈ in

¹/₄ in flat
washers

baseboard assembled
from two pieces of
mahogany glued
together

folded legs

self locking
nuts

block glued in
place to support
folded legs

2¹/₄ in x ³/₄ in x ¹/₂ in

⁵/₈ in

³/₄ in   ⁵/₈ in

¹/₄ in x 2 in brass plated
carriage bolts

1¹/₈ in

The Art of Wood Inlay

Inlay Procedure

1 Trace pattern ellipse on base wood and cut out with router, cut edges with chisel, and cut out center piece.

Routing out large oval for bed tray

Using wide chisel to cut edges of oval for inlay

Taking out center pieces of inlay cavity with chisel

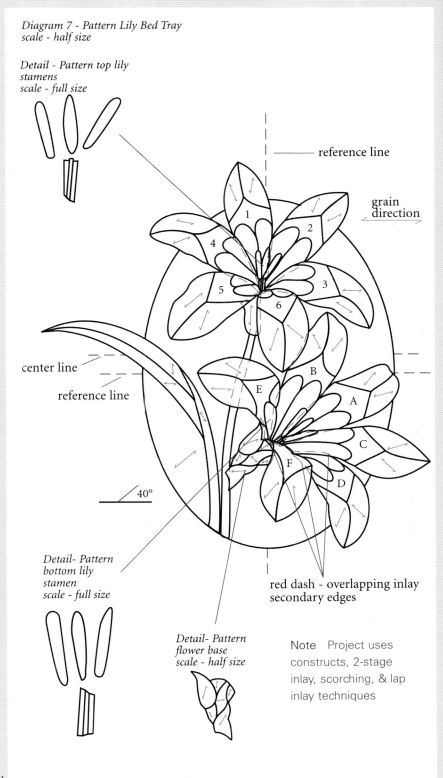

Diagram 7 - Pattern Lily Bed Tray
scale - half size

Detail - Pattern top lily
stamens
scale - full size

reference line

grain direction

center line

reference line

40°

1 2 3 4 5 6

A B C D E F

Detail- Pattern bottom lily stamen scale - full size

Detail- Pattern flower base scale - half size

red dash - overlapping inlay secondary edges

Note   Project uses constructs, 2-stage inlay, scorching, & lap inlay techniques

2 Make oval inlay from piece of mahogany, glue, and press into cavity.

3 To inlay the lily use a 2-stage procedure. First construct each petal separately. Fit and inlay each piece together (overlay style) in a separate block of wood (a sacrificial block, mahogany scraps). This way all primary edges that make up the internal definition of the petal can be made cleanly and with fine definition without struggling to fit each piece together manually. When all the internal edges are defined, cut the inlaid construct to its desired thickness. Place an accurately cut out pattern on the inlay assembled construct and trace the final petal shape, (use the cut-out pattern piece to help assemble the inlaid construct). Before you cut out each petal to its final shape it is important to decide the order in which you will inlay each petal (see diagram steps). You will also see from the diagrams that each petal is shaped with its base segments, where they join side by side to each other, cut with an appropriate secondary edge segment. It is easier to lap one inlay piece over another to achieve an accurate fit, than if you try to inlay each piece butt edge to butt edge (photo 6).

4 This project requires a different approach to the trimming flush of the inlay pieces. The working properties of each type of wood are sometimes quite different. The combining of several types into one project can sometimes create conflicts which require different solutions to make the project work.

5 The 3 main inlay woods used here are fairly hard and tight grained. This makes them easy to plane. Trimming the inlay pieces flush while constructing the lily petals in the sacrificial block becomes quick and easy because they are easily planed flush. The difficulty comes when you begin to inlay each petal into the tray bed. You cannot sand each petal flush. The fairly large segments of Ceylon ebony, if sanded, will turn the inlaid petal and the surrounding mahogany tray black. The very fine dust sanded from the ebony will fill the larger pores of the soft mahogany making it impossible to sand away. A cabinet scraper to shave the inlays flush also poses problems. Even if you inlay almost flush, the amount of material to be shaved away is considerable, counting the material from all 12 petals. Scraping the inlays flush will produce a very fine clean surface that will not be stained by the ebony or pao rosa, (also sometimes a problem). However, mahogany is almost impossible to scape without leaving small tears in its surface. The option of planing each petal flush with a small plane is also problematic. At any time, too much could be planed from the surface, leaving a hollow. To solve this problem use a power thickness planer set to the exact thickness of the tray. After inlaying each petal, pass

1 Petal parts -inlaid petal parts- finished shaped inlay construct cut from sacrificial block

2 Petal in sacrificial block, trim flush, stage 1 of two-stage inlay

3 Finished petal construct

4 Scorched edge defining center crease of petal

5 Walnut burl wood cut used for bottom inlay of lily

6 Placement of lily petal for step 2 of two-stage inlay (shows secondary edge on inlay petal)

Detail -construct of lower stamen

Caragana
Osage orange

7 Shaving inlays flush using power thickness planer

the tray through the planer to produce a clean shave for a perfectly flush tray. Repeating the operation after each inlay without altering the depth setting on the planer results in a finely finished inlay picture. If you choose a hardwood such as maple or oak in which to set the inlays, shaving the inlays flush is less difficult. Always make sure you know the proper direction to feed the tray through the planer before you start inlaying. Planing against the grain will leave a rough surface on the wood.

6 Constructing the flower base of this project can be achieved in several ways. Use the method you find easiest.

Make construct Assemble entire piece from small pieces of walnut before you start to inlay. Then inlay entire construct as one piece. (This is the method I used.)

Overlay Technique (see Yellow Rose Plaque) Cut each piece and inlay them in place overlay style. Each piece will have a primary and secondary, or minor edge segment. The last piece to be inlaid will have only primary edges, covering any remaining secondary edges.

Two-Stage Inlay This is the same method used to construct each lily petal. Assemble construct in a sacrificial block. Cut final inlay construct from block. Shape and re-inlay into tray.

Diagram 8- order of inlay of petal segments

1   2   3   4

5   6

5

Diagram 9A - top lily petals pattern & constructs
Pattern scale - half size
Construct scale - not to scale

grain
direction

to assist in assembling constructs of each lily petal, inlay each segment of each petal, overlay style, into a sacrificial block

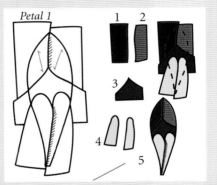

Petal 1

order of inlay of petal segments

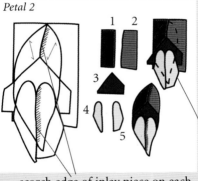

Petal 2

scorch edge of inlay piece on each petal to define contour seam (photo 4 on p118)

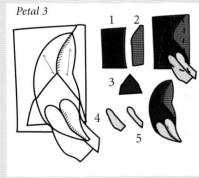

Petal 3

Trace the petal shape onto the inlaid segments & then cut out the final petal shape

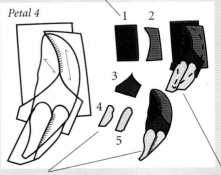

Petal 4

secondary segment

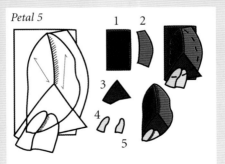

Petal 5

when cutting out petals from block, leave extra material on bottom section to allow overlay of each petal to its neighbor (photo 6 on p118)

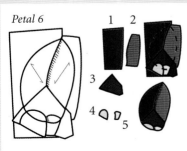

Petal 6

Lily Bed Tray

Diagram 9B - bottom lily petals pattern & constructs
Pattern scale - half size
Construct scale - not to scale

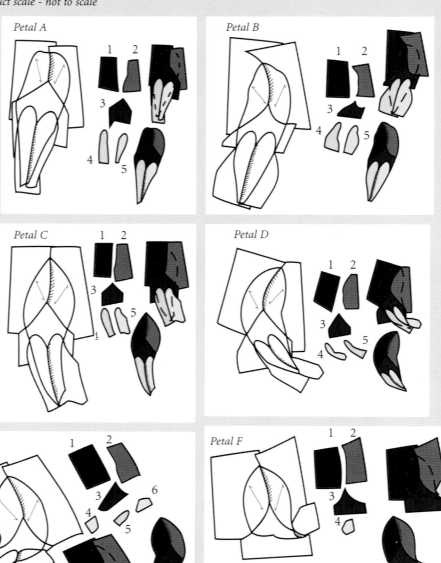

Petal A

Petal B

Petal C

Petal D

Petal E

Petal F

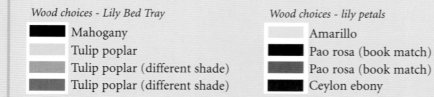

Wood choices - Lily Bed Tray
- ■ Mahogany
- ▨ Tulip poplar
- ▨ Tulip poplar (different shade)
- ▨ Tulip poplar (different shade)

Wood choices - lily petals
- ▢ Amarillo
- ■ Pao rosa (book match)
- ▨ Pao rosa (book match)
- ■ Ceylon ebony

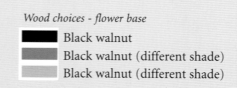

Wood choices - flower base
- ■ Black walnut
- ▨ Black walnut (different shade)
- ▨ Black walnut (different shade)

The Art of Wood Inlay

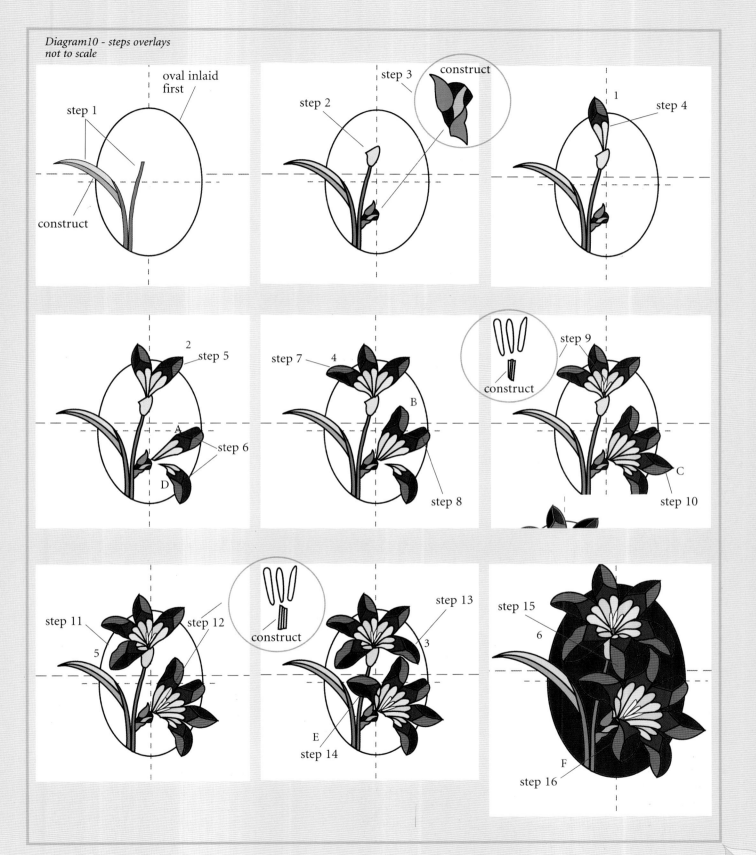

Diagram10 - steps overlays not to scale

step 1
construct
oval inlaid first

step 2
step 3
construct

1
step 4

2
step 5
A
D
step 6

step 7
4
B
step 8

construct
step 9
C
step 10

step 11
5
step 12
construct

step 13
3
E
step 14

step 15
6
F
step 16

Nested Bowls

T he interesting part of this project is that no router jig needs to be constructed. The initial freeform shape of the bowl is the only form required to complete the project. By following the steps outlined here, any freeform shape can be accommodated. You can easily add a few more pieces to the group.

Material

Hard maple 1 in x 6 in
Black walnut $1^7/_8$ in x 6 in

Note Thickness of black walnut required for the project is $1^1/_4$ in. I used a thicker piece which is less likely to split if the inlay (inset) is too tight. The walnut was trimmed to $1^1/_4$ in after the maple dish had been pressed onto place and before the final outside shape of the bowl was decided.

Bowl Construction

1 Using 1 in maple board carve out a freeform shape using straight cut router bit. Carve out 2 more bowls from maple board before cutting them free. This makes them easier to handle. See diagram 2. Trace the pattern lines shown in Diagram 1, onto the maple. The final inside dimension of the bowl will be this size plus $^1/_4$ in on all sides. Carve the bowl to a depth of $^{13}/_{16}$ in or less to achieve a finished depth of $1^7/_8$ in. See diagram 3A.

2 Create a rounded inside corner at the bottom of the bowl.

Note If you have $^1/_2$ in router and bit selection that includes a router bit that will perform the carving out of the bowl leaving a rounded bottom inside edge all in one operation, this step will not be necessary.

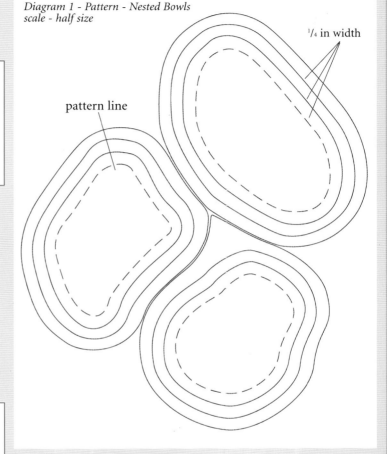

Diagram 1 - Pattern - Nested Bowls
scale - half size

$^1/_4$ in width

pattern line

Note Project uses deep inlay techniques

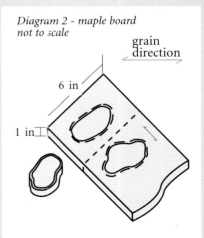

Diagram 2 - maple board
not to scale

grain direction

6 in

1 in

Cutting maple bowl lining
from rough stock

Two maple bowl sections

Scribing maple bowls onto
walnut stock

3 This work can be done using ³/₄ in core box router bit in a ¹/₄ in router, without having to construct a jig to restrain the router's motion while using this free cutting bit. Start cutting the edge by setting the core box bit ³/₁₆ in or less below top edge of the bowl. Allow the bit to undercut the edge until the shaft of the bit rides against the bowl's pattern marked edge (see diagram 3B).

4 Adjust the depth setting of the bit downward in small increments until the desired depth of ⁷/₈ in has been achieved. The greater the number of steps taken, the smoother the side of the bowl will be, leaving less to finish by sanding to complete the project. Carve the edges of the three pieces with each depth setting of the router bit. The bowl was routed only to ¹³/₁₆ in because if it was the full ⁷/₈ in, a small square corner would remain at the bottom inside edge when the core box bit also reached ⁷/₈ in (see diagram 3C).

5 Remove remaining material from the bottom of the bowl using the straight cut router bit. This thin layer is easily trimmed freehand. Leave a small ridge at the edge without allowing the router bit to mar the rounded corner (see diagram 3D).

6 Finish bowl bottom by hand with chisel and sandpaper (see diagram 3E).

7 The top inside edge of the bowl can now be finished. Use a ³/₁₆ in round over router bit fitted with a guide bearing. This will carve away the ¹/₄ in wide overhang. Finish rounding over the top edge (see diagram 3E).

8 Cut each bowl shape from the maple board with a power jigsaw. Cutting can be fairly rough. Finish shape using disk sander and spindle sander chucked into a drill press. Make sure all sides are parallel with each other and square to the bottom.

9 Place the maple bowl on the walnut block and scribe around as for any other inlay piece (see diagram 5A).

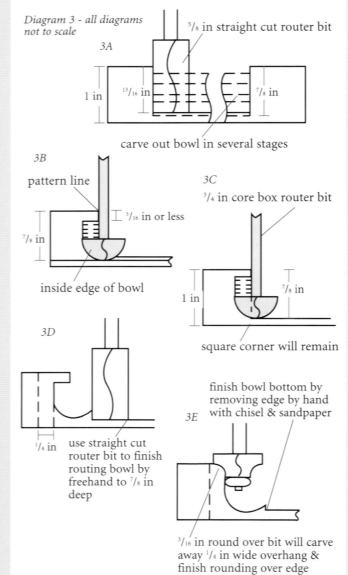

Diagram 3 - all diagrams not to scale

3A

⁵/₈ in straight cut router bit

1 in   ¹³/₁₆ in   ⁷/₈ in

carve out bowl in several stages

3B

pattern line

³/₁₆ in or less

⁷/₈ in

inside edge of bowl

3C

³/₄ in core box router bit

1 in   ⁷/₈ in

square corner will remain

3D

¹/₄ in   use straight cut router bit to finish routing bowl by freehand to ⁷/₈ in deep

3E

finish bowl bottom by removing edge by hand with chisel & sandpaper

³/₁₆ in round over bit will carve away ¹/₄ in wide overhang & finish rounding over edge

1 Release cut cutting into walnut - one maple shape almost cut to scribed line

2 Trimming walnut cavity back to scribed line

3 Maple bowl pressed into walnut cavity

4 Trimming walnut bowl to rough shape

The Art of Wood Inlay

10 Place the pieces 45° angle to each other to minimize stresses within the finished bowl structure (see diagram 4).

11 Using inlay knife, cut a shoulder on scribed line to clearly define its shape. Using a straight cutting router bit, rout out the cavity in the walnut down to a depth of 1 in in several stages, freehand. The more stages you use the easier the task. This will give a greater control of the router. Allow router to cut only what it will easily do, so you can have full control of the tool.

12 Cut the cavity as close to the scribe line as you can without cutting beyond the defined shape. Make sure the wood is secured firmly on your bench. It is also easier to carve all three pieces in a single board before they are cut apart. Finish cutting the vertical edges by hand with curved and straight chisels.

13 Stand a reference block of wood (which has been cut square with the surface) behind your chisel to give you a quick and accurate reference for your chisel position if required.

14 Maple and walnut bowl pieces can now be pressed together. Taper sides of the maple piece slightly. Taper up about ³/₄ in from the bottom edge. Cover all mating surfaces with white glue and proceed to press pieces together using a press block. I used three large C clamps equally spaced around the bowl and evenly tightened until the maple bowl was pressed to the bottom of the walnut cavity (see diagram 5C).

15 After separating each bowl by cutting them apart in almost a square shape, pass them through a table saw to trim to the desired 1¹/₄ in thickness. This is easily done if you have straight edges on the block (see diagram 5D).

16 Trim each maple walnut construct to the style grain or to any shape you choose that allows bowls to nest together.

17 Using a router mounted in a router table, finish the bowls' outside edges (see diagram 5E). Finish sanding each bowl thoroughly by hand and apply the finish of your choice.

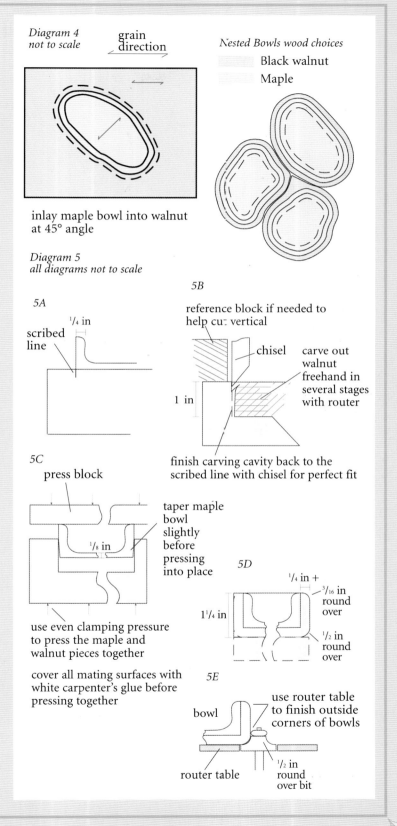

Diagram 4
not to scale

grain direction

inlay maple bowl into walnut at 45° angle

Nested Bowls wood choices

Black walnut

Maple

Diagram 5
all diagrams not to scale

5A

¹/₄ in

scribed line

5B

reference block if needed to help cut vertical

chisel

carve out walnut freehand in several stages with router

1 in

finish carving cavity back to the scribed line with chisel for perfect fit

5C

press block

¹/₈ in

taper maple bowl slightly before pressing into place

use even clamping pressure to press the maple and walnut pieces together

cover all mating surfaces with white carpenter's glue before pressing together

5D

¹/₄ in +

³/₁₆ in round over

1¹/₄ in

¹/₂ in round over

5E

bowl

use router table to finish outside corners of bowls

router table

¹/₂ in round over bit

Common Woods and Their Working Properties

Wood	1	2	3	4	5	6	7	8	9	10	11	12	Remarks
Ash	35	M	M	B	F	G	G	G 10-25	—	B 2/0	—	—	tough - hard to work with hand tools
Basswood	24	S	W	G	B	B	P	G 20-30	P	P—	P	F	excellent for trays, drafting boards
Beech	39	H	M	P	P	P	G	F 10-20	F	G 4/0	F	B	not durable outside, hard on tools because of mineral deposits
Birch	40	H	St	F	F	P	G	G 15-20	G	F 4/0	B	B	excellent for furniture, turning, dowels, handles
Butternut	25	S	W	B	G	F	P	G 10-25	G	F 4/0	F	F	furniture - perfect for walnut imitation
Cherry	36	M	M	G	B	F	P	B 10-25	B	B 4/0	B	B	furniture, handtrim, novelties
Chestnut	27	S	W	B	B	G	F	G 15-20	B	B 3/0	G	G	stains badly in contact with wet iron, v. dusty in all machining operations
Cottonwood	27	S	W	F	B	B	P	P 5-20	P	P 4/0	P	F	excellent for boxes & other nailing jobs - wears very well for softwood
Cypress	29	S	M	G	F	F	P	G 15-25	P	F 2/0	P	P	tends to splinter-most durable of Amer. woods for outdoor & soil exposure
Elm (Southern)	34	M	M	P	F	B	G	P 15-20	P	G 4/0	P	G	v. durable under paint - a good furn. wood despite difficulties in machining
Gum (Red)	33	M	M	P	B	G	F	F 10-20	B	F 4/0	F	F	one of most used furn. woods for imitations of walnut & mahogany
Hickory	43	H	St	G	G	P	G	G 10-25	G	B 2/0	F	B	excellent for furniture & steam bending, tool handles, wheels
Magnolia	30	S	W	F	B	B	B	G 5-15	F	G 4/0	G	P	excellent for steam bending, often marketed as poplar
Mahogany	35	M	M	B	B	G	P	G 5-25	B	G 4/0	B	B	one of the best furniture woods
Mahogany (Philippine)	33	M	M	B	B	G	P	G 5-25	G	P 3/0	F	F	generally coarser than true mahogany - furniture, boat planking, trim
(*) Maple (Hard)	41	H	St	G	F	P	F	F 15-20	G	G 4/0	B	B	fine furniture, flooring, turnings, dowling pins - one of best hardwoods
Maple (Soft)	31	M	M	F	G	F	F	P 10-15	F	G 4/0	F	P	some uses as hard maple but inferior wood - difficult to machine smooth
Oak (Red)	39	H	St	B	G	G	B	B 10-25	G	B 2/0	F	B	substitute for white oak in cheaper work
Oak (White)	40	H	St	B	G	G	B	B 10-20	G	B 2/0	G	B	interior trim, floors, furniture - one of most used American woods
Pine (White)	25	S	W	G	B	B	P	G 10-25	G	F 2/0	G	F	best all around softwood - excellent for paint
Pine (Yellow)	38	H	St	F	F	P	P	G 10-25	P	F 2/0	G	G	main uses - house construction, trim, floors
Poplar	29	S	W	G	B	B	F	G 5-20	G	P 4/0	P	F	excellent for carving, toys, corestock
Redwood	29	S	M	B	B	G	P	G 10-25	F	P 2/0	G	P	excellent for outdoor furniture, window stills, etc.
Sycamore	35	M	M	P	G	B	P	P 5-5	G	P 3/0	P	B	interior trim, furniture - difficult to machine but excellent appearance
Walnut	36	M	St	B	B	F	G	G 15-20	B	B 4/0	G	B	has very good feature for furniture & cabinet work

CODE: H=Hard M=Medium S=Soft St=Strong W=Weak B=Best G=Good F=Fair P=Poor

Note Data in this chart is largely from extensive tests made by U.S. Forest Products Laboratory, with some additions.

1 Weight -Pounds per cubic foot, dry. All woods vary in weight, even in the same tree from trunk to top.

2 Hardness

3 Strength - Composite strength value. woods rated weak are strong enough for all average work.

4 Stability - Rated on unrestrained value. Most woods are quite stable if properly seasoned and cared for.

5 Gluing

6 Nailing - Rated on ability to take nails near end without splitting.

7 Steam bending

8 Planing & Jointing - Flat grain stock, shallow cut. Rating runs at 15°, 20°, and 25° cutting angles. Bottom figure is best knife angle for smooth cutting.

9 Turning - Rated on smooth cutting and ability to hold detail. Not much difference between best and good.

10 Sanding - Rated on freedom from fuzz.

11 Shaping - Rated on smoothness of cut. Work speed decreases with hardness of wood which might be more importance than smoothness in production.

12 Mortising

* Sugar, white or hard maple. Distinguished from silver, red, big-leaf, or soft maple, an inferior machining wood, although often marketed simply as "maple."

The Art of Wood Inlay

Woods - Finishing Data

Wood	Natural Color	Usual Grain Figure	Stain type (1)	Stain color	Filler wt.(2)	Filler color	Bleach	Paint	Natural	Remarks
Alder (Red)	pink to brown	plain/figured	wipe/water	red/brown	none	none	y	y	y	1° Hardwood: Pacific coast-like red gum
Ash	gray to light.brown	cream sapwood	NGR	any	none	match wood	n	n	y pref.	same as red oak
Basswood	white to brown	plain/fiddleback	any	any	none/6	white/brown	y	y fill 1st	y	white filler-frosted finish(3)
Birch	cream	v. mild	NGR	red or brown	—	none	not nec.	y	n	fuzzy grain: muddy under oil stain
*Box Elder	cream	varied	water/wipe	maple	18	none	y	n interior	y	NGR w/wiping stain after sealer
Butternut	cream	mild	any	walnut/mahog	none	waln./mahog	y	y	y	used extensive. for walnut & mahog
Cedar	Heart amber Sap cream	like walnut	water	walnut/oak	8	med.brown	n	y	y	good for amber walnut w/out bleach
Cherry	Heart red Sap cream	knotty	none	none	14	none	n	n	y	red wiping stain to blend sapwood
Chestnut	red to brown	good	water	red/brown	none	red to black	n	y	y	excel. finish-good for brown mahog
Cypress	gray-brown	heavy grain	oil/wipe	red/brown	6-8	red/brown	n	y	y	large pores-good novelty finishes(3)
Ebony	d.brown to black	plain/stripe	NGR	d.red/brown	none	brown/black	n	n	y	oily-Gabson Ebony is blackest
Elm(Southern)	Heart amber Sap cream	plain/figured	water/oil/wipe	red/brown	15	none	n	y (6)	y	good for sand blast(4)-if stain-see(3)
Fir (Douglas)	brown to cream	heavy grain	water	red/brown	none/3	d.brown	n	y	y	cross-grain: hard to get even color
Gum (Red)	cream to red	plain/wild	wipe/oil	brown	12	none	n	y (7)	n	good-sand blast(4)-not pleasing stain
Hickory	white to cream	usually straight	water	red/brown	none	brown	y	n	y	good walnut/mahog.-blond finishes
Holly	Heart br.red Sap cream	plain/figured	any	red/brown	15	match wood	y	y	y	most-for waln. & mahog. imitations
Lacewood	silver white	mild	water	amber	none/3	none	not nec.	y	y	white wood: finish. natural
Magnolia	white to yellow	mild	oil/water	red/brown	none	none	n	y	n	usual. painted, satinwood imitation
Mahogany	med. brown	flake	water	oak/lt.walnut	none	d.brown	fairly wet	n	y	excel. cabinet wood-v. decorative
Mahogany (Philippine)	brown to red brown	stripe	water	red or brown	12	red to black	y	n	y	best cabinet wood-excel. finish
Maple (Hard)	brown to red brown	stripe	water/wipe	red or brown	12	red to black	y	n	y	NGR stain-minimizes grain-raising
Oak (English Brown)	deep brown	plain/flake/swirl	NGR	brown	none	browntoblack	y	y	y	cabinet wood - also "Pollard Oak"
Oak (Red)	red-brown	plain/flake	NGR	green toner(8)	15	brown	y	y	n	+bad grain-raising with water stain -hence NGR stain preferable
Oak (White)	white to lt. brown	plain/flake	NGR	brown	15	brown	y	y	n	- good for novelty finishes (3)
Orientalwood	lt .brown	stripe crossfire	water	amber/brown	12	brown	n	n	y	good water effects
Pine (White)	white to cream	mild	water(5)/oil	brown only	none	none	n	y	n	best for painting
Prima Vera	yellow-white	stripe crossfire	water	amber	12	natural/dark	y	y	y	"White Mahog."-excel. "blend" color
Redwood	red	mild st. grain	red only-tone	red only-tone	none	none	n	y	y	excel. exterior wood-best painted
Rosewood (Brazil)	red-brown	varied	NGR	red	15	d.red/black	n	n	y	oily-wash off w/ lacquer thinner before staining/finishing together
Rosewood (East Indies)	red-purple	stripe	NGR	d.red/red	12	d.red	n	n	y	
Sapeli	med. brown	stripe	water	brown	10	d.brown	n	n	y	v. similar to striped mahog.
Sycamore	white to pink	flake	water	amber/brown	none	none	seldom	y	y	good for natural finish
Walnut	Heart brown Sap cream	varied	water	walnut	14	browntoblack	y	n	y	obtainable in all figures
Zebra wood	tan w/ brown stripe	heavy stripe	water	light oak	12	natural	n	n	y	obvious grain-gives modern effects

*Box Elder (soft) - also known as Manitoba Maple

1 Where water stain is indicated, NGR (non-grain-raising) stain can also be used. "Oil" means penetrating oil stain. "Wipe" means wiping oil stain.

2 Pounds of filler paster per gallon of thinner.

3 All coarse-grain woods are good for novelty finishes, using contrasting filler, usually white.

4 Woods with alternate hard and soft streaks can be sand-blasted or burned with torch to cut out soft wood.

5 Water stains take better on resinous woods if wood is first sponged with 4 oz. sal soda and 1 oz. washing soda to gallon of water.

6 At 1 pt. benzol per gallon of paint for better penetration (primer only).

+7 Special sealers available to fill grain.

8 For brown tones, first spray weak green stain to kill red color of wood.

Index

acrylic finish, 21
aerosol can spray, 22
backyard inlay, 18, 44
basic bevel, 11
bench hook, 10, 91
bevels, 17, 61
bias cut, 81
black lacquered boxes, 4
bleeding, 21
bloom, 21
book matching, 18, 48, 54, 58, 73
bow tie inlay, 18
bracelet ornaments, 92
bulrush plaques, 32
bulrush plaques patterns, 33, 36, 38
burl, 8
butterflies, 18, 19
candle pattern, 112
candy dish, 43
candy dish pattern, 44
card box, 75
card box pattern, 76, 77
c-clamp, 61
cherries pattern, 41
chisels, 9
Christmas ornaments project, 107
Christmas ornaments pattern, 110, 111, 112
clamping blocks, 57
constructs, 18, 24, 27, 40, 48, 53, 58, 65, 69, 109, 118, 119, 120, 121
crow's foot, 9, 10, 35
daffodil pattern, 41
decorative tiles, 39
decorative tiles patterns, 40, 41, 42
deep inlay, 118
diamond stone, 11
double inlay, 18
drafting tools, 10
drawing inlay leaves, 15
drying time, 21
Dutchman, 19

earrings, brooch, bracelet project, 90
earrings, brooch, bracelet pattern, 92
electric motors, 9
end grain, 18, 69, 81
epoxy, 19, 21
ethyl alcohol, 21
files, 10
filtered exhaust systems, 21, 22
finishing, 20
finish types, 21, 22
fish eyes, 21
flat grain, 35
flat surface sanding, 20
flying Dutchman, 19
foam brush, 22
fruit tray, 71
fruit tray pattern, 72, 73
glue, 21
grapes tile pattern, 40
grinding, 11
hanger for plaque, 27
heartwood, 8
holly leaves pattern, 111
humidity, 21
inlay blocks, 13
inlay press, 10,13
inlay steps, 14, 17
inlay techniques, 18
inlay tools, 10
Japanese water stone, 11
lacquer, 22
laminated base, 18
lapped inlay, 18, 24, 27, 30, 34, 35, 40, 41, 42, 49, 69, 77, 81
lazy susan, 51
lazy susan pattern, 54
leaf constructs, 16, 24
leaf drawing, 15
leaf inlay, 16
lighting, 5, 21
lily bed tray project, 114
lily bed tray pattern, 115, 116, 117
mallet, 9

marquetry, 4
mushroom paddle trivet, 29
mushroom paddle trivet pattern, 30
napkin holder, 23
napkin holder patterns, 24, 25
nested bowls project, 122
nested bowls pattern, 123
non grain raising finish, 21
oily surface, 21
overlay, 18, 36
pattern transfer, 12
picture frame, 18
pin tray project, 103
pin tray project pattern, 105, 106
poinsettia plaque, 46
poinsettia plaque pattern, 47, 48, 49
poinsettia ornament pattern, 110
precatalyzed lacquer, 21
press block, 10, 69
primary bevel, 11
primary edge inlay, 18
recipe book stand, 63
recipe book stand pattern, 64, 66
recipe box, 59
recipe box pattern, 60, 62
red lacquered boxes, 4
repairing inlay, 19, 35
round acorn box, 84
round acorn box armature, 85, 86
round acorn box inlay, 89
round acorn box pattern, 89
round acorn box sanding jig, 87, 88
safety, 6, 22
sanding, 21, 22
sapwood, 8
scorching technique, 18, 27, 69
scraping tools, 10, 2
scribing, 54, 61
scratches, 20
sealer, 21, 22
secondary edge inlay, 18
shadow inlay, 18
sharpening tools, 11

shoulder cut, 17
spruce tree pattern, 111
striped frame, 33
spalting, 8
splitting wood, 13,
spray finish, 21, 22
swirling, 8
teddy bear step stool, 78
teddy bear step stool pattern, 79, 80, 81
thickness planer, 118
thicknessing, 34
tight inlay, 14
tree blossoms pattern, 42
trinket boxes, 55
trinket boxes pattern, 56, 57, 58
two-stage inlay, 18
ultraviolet light, 35
UV protection, 22
uneven finish, 21
varathane, 22
vegetable wall plaque, 26
vegetable wall plaque patterns, 27, 28
vertical edge, 17, 35
vise, 10, 13
walnut tulip plaque, 93
walnut tulip plaque pattern, 94, 95, 96
watering can tray, 67
watering can tray pattern, 69
wax surface, 21
white carpenter's glue, 10, 15
wood charts, 26, 27
wood combinations, 8
wood filler, 10, 35
wood grain, 8
woods to use, 6-8
work platform, 5
work space, 5
wrapped inlay, 18
wrapping techniques, 104
x-acto knife, 9
yellow rose plaque, 97
yellow rose plaque pattern, 100, 101, 102
yellow rose plaque template, 98, 97

METRIC EQUIVALENTS CHART (Inches to Millimeters and Centimeters)

MM=MILLIMETERS / CM=CENTIMETERS

INCHES	MM	CM	INCHES	CM	INCHES	CM
⅛	3	0.3	9	22.9	30	76.2
¼	6	0.6	10	25.4	31	78.7
⅜	10	1.0	11	27.9	32	81.3
½	13	1.3	12	30.5	33	83.8
⅝	16	1.6	13	33.0	34	86.4
¾	19	1.9	14	35.6	35	88.9
⅞	22	2.2	15	38.1	36	91.4
1	25	2.5	16	40.6	37	94.0
1¼	32	3.2	17	43.2	38	96.5
1½	38	3.8	18	45.7	39	99.1
1¾	44	4.4	19	48.3	48	101.6
2	51	5.1	20	50.8	41	104.1
2½	64	6.4	21	53.3	42	106.7
3	76	7.6	22	55.9	43	109.2
3½	89	8.9	23	58.4	44	111.8
4	102	10.2	24	61.0	45	114.3
4½	114	11.4	25	63.5	46	116.8
5	127	12.7	26	66.0	47	119.4
6	152	15.2	27	68.6	48	121.9